BHIMA SWARGA

3–

Overleaf: Young visitors under the painted ceiling of Kertha Gosa.

BHIMA SWARGA

The Balinese Journey of the Soul

IDANNA PUCCI

A BULFINCH PRESS BOOK

Little, Brown and Company • Boston • Toronto • London

Photography: Hans Hofer

Copyright © 1992 by Idanna Pucci

First Paperback Edition
First published in hardcover by Alfred van der Marck Editions 1985

Most of the photography in this book is the work of Hans Hofer.
Other photographs are by Idanna Pucci (page 17); and Brent Hesselyn
(page 27); the top map on page 8 is reproduced courtesy of the
Harvard College Library; the drawing by William Blake on page 11
is reproduced courtesy of the Fogg Museum, Harvard University
Bequest–Grenville L. Winthrop; Max Lawrence reproduced the
photograph on page 19 (courtesy of Dr. Willard A. Hanna and the
private collection of Puri Karangasem); the photograph by Walter Spies
on page 20 is reproduced courtesy of the Kon. Instituut v/d Tropen,
Amsterdam; all other photographs and art-works are reproduced
by permission of Hans Hoefer and the Apa Archives, Singapore.

Library of Congress Cataloging-in-Publication Data
Pucci, Idanna, 1945–
    [Epic of life]
    Bhima swarga: a Balinese journey of the soul/Idanna Pucci.—
    1st pbk. ed.
    p.   cm.
    Originally published: The epic of life. 1st ed. c1985.
    "A Bulfinch Press book."
    Includes bibliographical references (p.   ).
    ISBN 0-8212-1896-4
    1. Bhima swarga—Illustrations.   2. Ceilings—Indonesia—Bali
    (Province)   3. Painting, Hindu—Indonesia—Bali (Province)
    4. Hinduism—Indonesia—Bali (Province) I. Bhima swarga.
    English. 1992. II. Title.
    ND2840.B3P8 1992
    751.7′3′095986—dc20   91-32371

Bulfinch Press is an imprint and trademark of Little, Brown and
    Company (Inc.)
Published simultaneously in Canada by Little, Brown & Company
    (Canada) Limited

PRINTED IN SINGAPORE

*To the Balinese clowns Twalen and Mredah, the
principal characters of this book, in the hope that
I, too, once on the "other side," will become as
courageous as they*

Acknowledgments

To Dr. Barbara Stoler Miller, professor of Oriental studies at Barnard College, Columbia University, who believed from the very start in the value and quality of my work.

In Bali, to Putu Budiastra, director of the Bali Museum; David Stuart-Fox, scholar of Balinese religion; the late Australian artist Donald Friend, whose talent as a storyteller greatly inspired me; Wija and Tatie Wawo-Runtu, Made Wijaya, Brent Hesselyn, Pino Confessa, and John Darling; I Made Kichen; Ida Bagus Pt. Badra; I Made Kanta; Mangku Mura; I Nyoman Oka; A.A.G. Rai; I Gusti Gde Raka from Saba; Tjokorda Gde Dangin from Sidemen; and the many, many Balinese people who participated in my work and life.

In New York, to Susan Bergholz, editor, for her sensitivity to myth and the "story"; Vidya Dehejia, art historian, and Dr. Willard A. Hanna, historian of Indonesia, for their valuable advice; and to Dr. Jan Fontein, of the Boston Museum of Fine Arts, for his enthusiastic support.

In Paris, to Hugues de Montalembert, with whom I first discovered Bali and who, early in my life, taught me how to use my eyes in a more profound way so as to see the truly amusing, absurd and significant sides of life; and to Luc Bouchage for his early encouragement.

To the friends who believe in me and have helped me with advice: Roberto Gerosa; Nicolette Jelen; Bernard de Bonnerive; Carole Wyman; Brian McGarry; Camilla d'Afflitto; Mimma Marescalchi; Shirley Kennedy; Claudia Ruspoli; George Schwartz; Alvise and Carla Alverà; Sharon Kitagawa; Simone di Bagno; and Ivo J. Lederer.

To my family: my father, Puccio Pucci; my mother, Marina Piccolomini, with Antonio and Micaela; and my brother, Giannozzo.

And to Hans Hoefer, who gave me the beautiful photographs for this book as homage to the friendship we shared throughout the years of my adventure with Kertha Gosa and Bhima Swarga.

Idanna Pucci

An old map of the Indonesian archipelago, showing Bali, a tiny island directly east of "Java," in the lower center section.

The island of Bali, showing key villages and towns important to the history of Kertha Gosa.

JAVA SEA • Singaraja

BALI Karangasem •
• Klungkung
Ubud • • Kamasan
• Gelgel

INDONESIAN OCEAN • Denpasar

8

INTRODUCTION

*What at first glance is further from the Florence of Marsilio
Ficino than Calcutta and Benares? . . . Nevertheless, I found
myself there because, as was the case with the humanists
of the Renaissance, a provincial image of man did not satisfy
me, and because, ultimately, I dreamed of rediscovering the
model of a "universal man."*

—*Mircea Eliade,*
No Souvenirs, 1957–1969

This book is the result of a very personal relationship
with a work of art. Like the very circumstances out of
which the book was born, it represents a singular experience at a time and in a place—an experience that not
even I can ever hope to repeat. As such it is not the work
of a professional scholar of literature or of a trained art
historian, but of a storyteller who happened to fall in
love with a masterpiece of classical Balinese art. I did not
reflect on the controversial difficulties inherent in every
translation of an Eastern work into Western form, or on
the complex matter of transposing an oral tradition to
a literary one, or, furthermore, on the fact that the story
depicted on the ceiling of Kertha Gosa is an offshoot of
an oral experience expressed through the medium of
visual art, and that this fact alone is alive with dangerous
ambiguities. Had I been a trained scholar, and therefore
conscious of all the implications of these difficulties,
I might have embarked on this adventure in a very
different way.

This book, therefore, should not be viewed as the
ultimate wisdom on the paintings of Kertha Gosa—
although I do hope that it will contribute to scholarship—
but rather as the work of a storyteller, fascinated with
the wondrous mysteries of the human condition, with the
wisdom transmitted through the ephemeral method of
word of mouth and, in this particular case, through
both word of mouth and "image of eye." During the
moment this "transmission" happens it is real and tangible.
When this singular event at a time and in a place is over,
it becomes like a dream or an illusion, living on only in
one's own imagination.

The following notes are an attempt to inform the
reader about the nature of my adventure, the unusual
process of my research and the circumstances out of
which this book was born.

The tiny island of Bali, lying immediately to the east
of Java and appearing as a minute speck in the Indonesian
archipelago, is a complete universe unto itself, a micro-
cosm of Hindu culture in the midst of a Muslim-dominated
world. When I first arrived in Bali, in December 1973, I
found that not only did it satisfy all the expectations my
imagination had conjured up but that, in fact, it far
exceeded them. As my readings about the island had led
me to anticipate, Balinese life is still permeated by belief
in a divine, omnipresent force. In every gesture of a
musician playing his *gamelan* instrument, in every whirl
of a temple dancer, in every motion of a farmer sowing a
rice field, in every shadow cast by a puppet in a shadow
play, the Balinese perceive a manifestation of this super-
natural power. The paintings and wood carvings, the
stone sculptures and temples that dominate the landscape
of daily life in Bali are not merely artistic reflections
of a rich cultural heritage but are, in fact, an organic
outgrowth of the people themselves, a special dimension
of their being—as natural a part of them as their hands
or eyes. In Bali, the gap between "myth" and "reality"
does not seem to exist. The religious, the mythological, is
acted out in life. It seems to grow spontaneously, with the
same lushness as the vegetation itself. During a shadow-
play performance, the Balinese do not regard the characters merely as entertaining puppets but endow them with
flesh and blood and identify with them completely. The
tales of the *Ramayana* and the *Mahabharata,* the great
Hindu epics, are embedded in the psyche of every Balinese,
whether peasant or prince.

Living among the Balinese on and off for over six
years put me in daily contact with a society that I only
began to make sense of slowly.

The Balinese are Hindu—a fascinating phenomenon,
considering that the rest of Indonesia has been so strongly
influenced by Islam—and traditional Hindu society

exhibits one of the clearest examples of hierarchical stratification in the world today. However, the Balinese have evolved a form of Hinduism that differs in many ways from that of India—a form that appears to be less rigid in its structure.

Traditionally, each person's *dharma*, or duty in life, is delineated by his hereditary social class, and one of the gravest infractions of the law is to cross the boundaries of one's own class. What to the Westerner appears as a rigidity that stifles individualism, the traditional Hindu regards as a perfectly natural reflection of the cosmic order of things. Just as each of the four elements—fire, air, water and earth—and each of the four seasons—spring, summer, autumn and winter—is assigned its own special and necessary function in the natural cycle, so in precisely the same way each of the four castes is entrusted with its own sacred responsibility: *brahmins* are the priests, the learned spiritual leaders; *ksatrias,* the warriors and nobles, the secular rulers; *vaishyas,* the merchants and businessmen; and *sudras,* the farmers and laborers, who perform the other menial tasks which are absolutely necessary for society.

In Bali, the four-caste division is not so rigorously delineated as in India:* the *brahmana, satria* and *wesia* castes tend to form a group of their own, referred to as the *triwangsa,* while the rest of the population belongs to the *sudra* class.[1] Far from agitating against the inequity of such a hierarchy, the traditional Balinese possess such a deep, implicit faith that their society is the earthly manifestation of the divine, universal truth that they consider it their holy duty to fulfill whatever this earthly hierarchy, the mirror of the gods' own hierarchy, requires of them. If they do not, they believe the effects of their error will not only tarnish their own individual *karma* (an accumulation of deeds that accompanies them through every successive incarnation) but will also reverberate throughout the universe, resulting in cosmic chaos.

The sense of belonging to a group, of communal identification, is so deeply ingrained in the Balinese from infancy onward at every level of human interaction that

their capacity and desire to blend harmoniously with the group is virtually instinctual. However, Balinese society, which in one sense absorbs the individual, in another sense emphasizes individuality to a great degree. Going hand in hand with the idea of *karma,* whereby a person is responsible for his or her own destiny—literally "making" or "unmaking" oneself—is the implicit assumption that the individual alone must effect his or her own salvation. In Hindu terms, this is tantamount to realizing the Self, the universal force (*Brahman*) that dwells at the center of every individual's being. The soteriological function is assigned not to a redeemer figure who, literally through divine grace, will rescue a soul from eternal damnation but, rather, to each individual.

The most obvious differences between Balinese Hinduism and present-day Hinduism in India are that there is no untouchability in Bali, no cow worship (the Balinese, except for the priests, eat beef) and less prudery, and men and women interact much more freely and treat one another as equals (widows sometimes remarry, and women may divorce).

The most important feature of Bali's communal ethos—not unique to Bali, but belonging in some degree to any traditional society—is the sanctity of the family. For example, a woman who is barren (even if through no fault of her own) is looked down upon, and a man who has produced no offspring is considered, figuratively, to have remained a child for his entire life because he has not been able to replace his childhood name with a "real" man's customary name, "father of . . . ."[2] Similarly, spinsters and bachelors are looked upon with reproach. Marriage is the social norm and therefore "required," mainly because in popular belief the great-grandparent is normally reincarnated as the great-grandchild. In Bali, therefore, social legitimatization cannot be achieved without proof of fertility. Sterility is interpreted as a threat to social equilibrium, to the possibility of reincarnation, and consequently to the equilibrium of the entire universe.

As one would expect in such a family-oriented culture, parents are accorded the utmost respect. By the same

token, every newborn baby is believed to come into this world directly from Heaven and is therefore treated with the reverence due a god.

This picture of Balinese society arose from my experience of observing the Balinese while sharing their daily life.

Then, one day I visited Klungkung, Bali's former nominal royal capital, and there, in a building called Kertha Gosa (a name literally meaning "the place where the king meets with his ministers to discuss questions of justice") I was utterly overwhelmed by the paintings I saw on its ceiling. Although I knew nothing about the subject matter of these paintings, I was astonished by what were clearly depictions of an enormous variety of punishments—in graphic, gruesome detail. I recall how Dante and his *Divine Comedy* came to mind. This was

perhaps a normal reaction for a Florentine finding herself gazing at a Balinese ceiling with the same awe and wonderment with which, as a schoolgirl in Florence many years earlier, she had listened to a nun's voice describing, with what seemed perverse relish, every horrific detail of Dante's vision of Hell and Purgatory.

After that day, my curiosity about these Balinese paintings grew until it took the form of an obsession. I began researching Kertha Gosa, but could find no specific information about it other than a short paragraph in Miguel Covarrubias's classic book *Island of Bali* mentioning that the pavilion of Kertha Gosa had served as a court of justice and that the story painted on its ceiling was called *Bhima Swarga.*

This legend, I learned, is an offshoot of the great Indian classic the *Mahabharata,* which one might call the

Hindu counterpart of Homer's *Iliad.* This epic cannot be dated with any certainty. It developed gradually between 400 B.C. and A.D. 400, undergoing the elaborations common to epics in an oral tradition. Although a great many anonymous authors undoubtedly contributed to the composition of the *Mahabharata,* the poet Vyasa is often credited with its compilation. Consisting of 100,000 verses, the *Mahabharata* deals mainly with a war of succession between two royal families, the Pandavas (five brothers, of whom Bhima is one) and their cousins, the Kauravas,[3] who struggle over the rulership of the ancient kingdom of Kuru in northern India. It is essentially a moral epic, extolling the rectitude, wisdom and perseverance of the noble *satria* caste and stressing integrity, filial devotion and the ultimate triumph of virtue over vice. For centuries, the *Mahabharata* has held a central place in Indian culture; even today it is recited to huge audiences just as it was hundreds of years ago—for it is said, "He who with fervid devotion listens to a recitation of the *Mahabharata* attains [hereafter] to high success in consequence of the merit that becomes his through understanding even a very small portion thereof. All the sins of that man who recites or listens to this history with devotion are washed off."[4]

The *Mahabharata* came to the island of Bali by way of eastern Java, which is separated from Bali by only a narrow strait. According to old Javanese records, the first translations of the epic from Sanskrit into Kawi, the ancient Javanese language, appear to have been made about A.D. 900, during the reign of Dharmawangsa. The epic was gradually transmitted to Bali, probably between the years 1019 and 1042, when eastern Java was ruled by Dharmawangsa's nephew, Airlangga, one of the greatest monarchs of ancient Java. By this time Java had already been under Hindu and Buddhist influences for more than 400 years. Airlangga's mother took as her second husband a prince of Bali, and that was the formal connection that seems to have opened Bali to cultural exchange with Hindu Java.

But the massive cultural penetration of the island came three centuries later, in the year 1343, with the conquest of Bali by the Hindu-Javanese Majapahit dynasty. The Hindu-Balinese trace their original ancestors to members of the Majapahit court and army who took possession of their island in the fourteenth century.

As Islam overwhelmed the Hinduism of Java in its eastern sweep, resulting in the establishment of the Muslim state of Mataram in the sixteenth century, the local rulers of Java adopted the new religion and proclaimed themselves sultans. The Hindu princes of Bali, however, remained untouched by Islam. How and why Bali managed to develop and preserve the Hindu culture and religion over the centuries, during which most of Indonesia became a bastion of Islam, is an intriguing historical puzzle to which there are no fully satisfactory answers. Perhaps the most persuasive explanation is advanced by the anthropologist Clifford Geertz, who finds great significance in the geographic position of Bali. In his view, Bali lay outside the mainstream of the spice trade that exploded in this part of the world in the sixteenth and seventeenth centuries. "Bali," states Geertz, "faced south toward the Indian ocean where, given poor harbors and rough seas, there was hardly any trade, rather than north toward the Java Sea, the Asian Mediterranean around which Chinese, Indian, Arabic, Javanese, Buginese, Malay and European merchants shuttled like so many itinerant peddlers. Much of Bali's reputation for seclusion and isolation stems from this fact."[5]

It is thus that the *Mahabharata* came to be incorporated into Balinese culture. Its influence is felt in several art forms: dance, drama, wood carving, sculpture, painting and the plots of the *wayang kulit,* or shadow-puppet theater.

In Bali, however, the Indian title *Mahabharata* has never been formally employed; instead, the eighteen sections (*parvas*) of the epic are treated as independent episodes—each a story unto itself, with its own title. Moreover, through the centuries, the Balinese came to emphasize the dramatic aspects of the exciting exploits of the several major heroes, rather than the more sophisticated philosophical nuances of the original Indian epic. The *dalangs* (shadow-play puppeteers), in particular, have been central catalysts for the popularization and secularization of the individual stories, although painters, sculptors and dancers have also been important. Whatever the medium, the various episodes of the *Mahabharata* transmit their inherent traditional ethical values and aesthetic codes to the popular consciousness. In Bali, the traditional stories are a mirror of both the worldly and the spiritual concerns of the people. There are obvious parallels between the impact of these epic stories on everyday life in Bali and the impact of Old Testament heroes and villains on life in medieval Europe. But while such figures as Lot, David and Goliath have lost much of their immediacy in the modern West, Bhima and his brothers are alive on the Balinese stage.

The story of *Bhima Swarga* is a particularly fascinating case in point. The title itself illustrates, linguistically, a departure from the original Sanskrit conception: it is an abbreviated form of *Bhima ka Swarga,* which in Balinese means literally "Bhima goes to the abode of the gods." *Swarga* refers to *any* place where the deities happen to reside, whether Heaven or Hell. The original Sanskrit *Svarga* is a term reserved exclusively for Heaven and never used in connection with Hell, which is called *Naraka.* Curiously enough, the Balinese tale of "Bhima goes to the abode of the gods" cannot be found in the Sanskrit *Mahabharata.* The only feature of the original related at all to this story is a brief passage in the epic's final portion, *Svargarohanika,* describing the journey, not of Bhima but of his elder brother Yudhisthira, to Svarga on a mission quite different from that of Bhima in the *Bhima Swarga.*[6] Clearly, *Bhima Swarga* is purely a creation of the Balinese popular imagination.

Stripped of all its marvelous details, the story's basic plot is quite simple. Bhima, second oldest of the five Pandawa brothers, is charged by his mother Kunti with the mission of rescuing from Hell the souls of his earthly father, Pandu, and his second mother, Madri.* After saving them from Hell, he must secure their admission

*In Bali, Pandu's second wife becomes Bhima's second mother.

to Heaven, which involves the ordinarily impossible task of wresting from the gods the water of immortality (Tirta Amrta) for them to drink. Throughout his journey to both Hell and Heaven, his two loyal servants, or "aides-de-camp," accompany him. These strictly Balinese inventions figure, in actuality, as the central characters of the story, for they represent the ordinary Balinese, and it is with them that the people identify.

The reason for doing a book about the *Bhima Swarga* story depicted on the ceiling of Kertha Gosa was not to record the history of yet another monument. The idea came alive gradually, the inevitable result of my questions. In fact, without being fully aware of what I was getting into, I found myself caught up in the process of unraveling the "mystery" of these paintings. Not only their beauty, but their universal human message, had profoundly moved me. Ultimately, I devoted an important period of my life to this fascinating Balinese work of art; I was propelled into it and carried along by sheer curiosity, by a strange feeling of identification and by the immense pleasure I found in the difficult process of the search itself. The fundamental questions that motivated me were the obvious ones: What did these paintings *really* represent? How had they been made? By whom? And, most of all, why did they appear on this particular ceiling?

Finding out what Kertha Gosa was about was like trying to reconstruct a puzzle, the pieces of which had been lost over time. The entire experience operated on different levels simultaneously. Luckily, in a culture as alive and self-renewing as that of Bali, nothing ultimately is lost. Everything is always present and therefore does not need to be frozen in time or recorded for the future. If religion is alive and deeply felt, then culture is alive as well. History intermingles with religion, and religion with art, and art is life.

Although my research fed on these same timeless qualities, with nothing ever completely certain to hold onto and the facts of history mingling at all times with more esoteric and differing interpretations of the paintings, I will try to introduce Kertha Gosa to the reader as

*Painted ceiling
of Kertha Gosa.*

one introduces a special person: first by describing the appearance, the features, the outward personality, and only afterward by uncovering the inner character.

Kertha Gosa and the History of Klungkung

Entering Kertha Gosa and gazing at the ceiling for the first time, one is struck not so much by the individual paintings as by the impact of the ceiling as a whole—its colors, figures and lavish patterns.

From the apex of Kertha Gosa's roof, four equilateral triangles slope downward so that their bases, each 33 feet (10 meters) long, join at right angles to form a perfect square. Covering the ceiling are a total of 267 panels of polychrome paintings in the traditional *wayang* style,

arranged in nine rows depicting four different sets of narrative material.

On the lowest level of the ceiling is a row of small narrative panels with five stories from the *Tantri* repertory.[7] Above this begins the main feature of Kertha Gosa: the story of *Bhima Swarga,* which occupies five rows and reads clockwise, starting at the far northeastern corner of the ceiling. The first two rows of the *Bhima Swarga* paintings represent Bhima's exploits in Hell; and the top three rows, his journey to Heaven. Separating these two sets of adventures—that is, between Hell and Heaven— are intervening rows of panels that afford a pause, an "intermission," in the *Bhima Swarga* narrative. In the first row of these panels is illustrated a story from *Adiparwa*[8]; and in the second row, the Balinese astrological calendar *pelelingtangan.*[9] The panels of the ceiling's last three rows, dealing with the Heaven portion of *Bhima Swarga,* decrease in number as the ceiling rises and narrows. The narrative sequence culminates in the ceiling's four largest panels—trapezoidal in shape and situated at the roof's peak—representing Heaven, with a god at each of the four cardinal points.

At the center of the ceiling, in the square space formed where the upper edges of these four panels join at right angles, there is a lotus surrounded by four doves, an auspicious motif carved from wood and covered with gilt, symbolizing good fortune, enlightenment and ultimate salvation.

When, why and by whom was this ceiling painted? The only available data allow us to sketch a rough historical outline relating to the Kertha Gosa pavilion itself but not to its ceiling paintings. When the palace of Klungkung —Bali's former nominal royal capital, located 26 miles east of the present capital, Denpasar—was built in the early eighteenth century under the Dewa Agung Gusti Sideman, first *raja* of Klungkung, the pavilion of Kertha Gosa quite probably was constructed at the same time. Since Kertha Gosa is located at the most sacred corner of the entire palace compound, nearest to the holy volcano Gunung Agung, we can be reasonably certain that the pavilion played a prominent role in the life of the *raja* and the entire palace community. It is highly unlikely that this most sacred site would have been left unoccupied when the compound was first built; therefore Kertha Gosa must have been part of the original palace complex.

As the seat of the Dewa Agung—the highest of all Balinese royal titles—Klungkung became both the nominal and the cultural center of Bali after 1710.[10] Prior to that date, Bali's ancient capital had been approximately three miles south of Klungkung at Gelgel, toward the sea, where the most prominent line of Balinese rulers had finally settled after the Majapahit Javanese conquest of the island.

Although the invading *brahmana* and *satria* of the Majapahit dynasty had divided the island into several kingdoms, they were, like feudal lords, still subject to the Dewa Agung of Gelgel, who as the most direct descendant of the Majapahit rulers ranked highest among the Balinese kings.

When Dalem Dimade inherited the title of Dewa Agung in 1665, Gelgel entered a period of turmoil. Dimade ordered his prime minister, I Gusti Agung Maruti, to reconquer the island of Lombok, east of Bali, which, aided by the Sultan of Makassar in the Celebes, had rebelled against Gelgel. A fine general, Maruti won back the island in 1678. But when he sent three members of his family to report the good news to the Dewa Agung, the king, fearing Maruti's ambition, had them executed. In revenge, the furious Maruti, with troops from reconquered Lombok, soon launched an attack on Gelgel, causing the Dewa Agung to flee. Maruti then proclaimed himself *raja* in 1686.

Several Balinese kings, notably the lords of Badung (now Denpasar) and Buleleng, refused to accept the sovereignty of Maruti and helped Dimade to regain his throne in 1705. At Dimade's death, a year or two later, the title of Dewa Agung passed to his son, Gusti Sideman, who for superstitious reasons transferred the court from Gelgel to nearby Klungkung in 1710.

A patron of the arts, the Dewa Agung Gusti Sideman took great pains in supervising the design and construction of his palace at Klungkung, the Puri Semara Pura, with the result that this royal compound stood out as an artistic jewel, an exquisite example of Hindu-Balinese architecture. Like all the Balinese kings, Gusti Sideman insisted on utilizing only the finest workmen and materials in building and decorating his palace. Masters of wood carving, painting and sculpture, silversmiths and goldsmiths, musicians and dancers, formed an integral part of court life. Here the traditional Balinese style of architecture and painting reached full maturity. During his reign, Kamasan, the nearby village of painters that had previously rendered service to Gelgel, became officially linked with the court of Klungkung. The flowering of Kamasan painting can be attributed to Gusti Sideman's patronage.

The splendor of the Klungkung palace exemplified

a trend seen in other courts throughout Bali during this era: a predilection for artistic precision, excellence and opulence. With the encouragement of these courts, artists blended the inherited Hindu-Javanese Majapahit motifs and techniques with indigenous forms, thereby evolving a genuinely Balinese art. It is noteworthy that during this same period—the golden age of Balinese art—other aspects of Hindu-Javanese Majapahit culture, particularly religion and philosophy, became fully localized as well, mingling with native pre-Hindu animistic practices and beliefs.

The palace of Klungkung was laid out in a square, each of the sides measuring 500 feet (150 meters). Viewed from above, the palace compound presumably took the overall shape of a *mandala,* for it was designed as a microcosmic reflection of the macrocosm.

Within the compound were numerous courtyards, gardens and moats surrounding several *bales* (typical Balinese buildings, partly of masonry and partly of wood), with each *bale* serving a particular function. The sacred precinct of the palace complex, reserved for rituals and ceremonies celebrating the unity between men and gods, was distinctly separate from the areas associated with everyday life.[11]

Among the *bales* erected in the sacred area two

seemed of particular importance—the *bale* of Kertha Gosa and the *bale* Kambang, or "floating pavilion," both of which stood in the Taman Agung, or "sacred garden," later renamed Taman Gili, or "garden with moats." Adjacent to the wall separating the palace compound from the town's main intersection (where today the street Raja Gelgel meets the street Raja Suyapati), this garden extended on the east side of the main gate to the palace. Its frangipani, hibiscus and varied tropical plants were used as offerings to the gods, and its moats, which can still be seen, were filled with floating lotus flowers.

The rectangular *bale* Kambang, at the center of the Taman Gili, served not only as the royal guards' headquarters but also as the antechamber for the *raja's* visitors. Originally smaller than it is today, under the Dutch this *bale* was restored and enlarged to its present size. Its ceiling is intricately decorated with eight rows of narrative paintings in the traditional *wayang* style. Beginning from the bottom, the first row consists of paintings from Balinese astrology; the next row shows the children's tale of *Pan Brayut,* the story of a couple who had eighteen children; and the remaining rows depict various stories about Sang Sutasoma, the archetypal wise old man of Balinese folklore.

At the far eastern corner of the Taman Gili, the *bale*

View of the bale *Kambang with Kertha Gosa in the background.*

Kertha Gosa is situated in the center of Klungkung, former royal capital of Bali.

of Kertha Gosa was erected in the most sacred area of the palace compound. From the high Kertha Gosa pavilion, the *raja* has a clear view of his palace as well as a panorama of the town and all the surrounding land. Sometimes he would note a pretty girl on her way to market or to the temple with offerings. He would then whisper an order to an aide kneeling at his feet, and the girl would soon disappear behind the palace walls, later to reappear as one of the many royal wives.

High up on Kertha Gosa, the *raja* would retreat to listen privately to a high priest (*padanda*) read aloud from a *lontar,* a sacred book etched on palm leaves, containing philosophical teachings of the ancient Hindu doctrines.

The Kertha Gosa pavilion's major function, however, pertained to matters of justice. It was there that the *raja* met with the *brahmana* judges (*kerthas*) to discuss issues of the law and human affairs. These would include cases of political conspiracy, special status infringement, ritual sacrilege, adultery, or the elopement of a commoner with the daughter or son of a *brahman* (still taboo among

the Balinese, for it is believed to pollute both the high- and low-caste families). Most such legal and social issues involved problems within the aristocratic strata of the kingdom, since the majority of cases—both criminal and civil—concerning villagers were resolved by the village priests themselves without prior consultation with the *raja.* In Bali the village priests, in discussing a case with the council of village elders, always acted as judges. Only in rare, important instances was a case dealing with villagers brought to royal attention and discussed at Kertha Gosa. When this occurred, three judges presided over the meeting, in addition to the *raja* himself.

During the centuries when Klungkung's royal family reigned supreme, Kertha Gosa was not a court of justice in the Western sense—that is, a tribunal where trials take place in the presence of the accused. It would have been inconceivable to permit a "criminal" to enter the sacred area, or, for that matter, *any* area of any royal palace, let alone the palace of the highest-ranking ruler of Bali, the Dewa Agung of Klungkung. This would have caused spiritual and social pollution affecting not only the king, his palace and the entire court but also the entire kingdom.

This much, then, can be ascertained as reasonably accurate historical background for the Kertha Gosa pavilion; but when we approach the issue of the pavilion's elaborate ceiling decoration, we find little concrete information.

Whether or not the king instructed his court painters from Kamasan to decorate the ceiling at the time Kertha Gosa was built is impossible to know with certainty. It is all but impossible to determine exactly when the ceiling was first painted, and also whether or not the story of *Bhima Swarga* was the subject of the first paintings. The earliest and, in fact, the only record of any paintings at Kertha Gosa dates from the year 1842 and is written in a *lontar* that belongs to the historical library, the Gedong Kirtya, in Singaraja.[12] Its author extols the beauty of Kertha Gosa's decorations, but does not discuss the subject matter depicted on the ceiling; nor does he mention whether the paintings were a permanent feature of the pavilion or if they had simply been installed temporarily for the celebration he describes.

It is plausible that the *raja* might have deemed the story of *Bhima Swarga,* dealing as it does with moral and social questions and with justice in general, an appropriate subject for the ceiling of a pavilion where he and his ministers considered these very questions and attempted to administer justice. But this is pure speculation, which cannot be supported by any firm evidence. The Kertha Gosa ceiling decoration is unique, for in Bali the *Bhima Swarga* legend normally occurs only in connection with death: it appears, for instance, in the form of narrative sculpture on the walls of some temples dedicated to Durga,[13] the goddess of death, and the story is usually recited by priests and *dalangs* on the eve of a cremation.

It is probable, then, that if any paintings were executed especially for Kertha Gosa, they were made on cloth and were either of two types: *ulan-ulan,* paintings attached to a wooden surface, or *ider-ider,* which are customarily hung around the eaves of ritual *bales* or small temples. Furthermore, we can speculate that these paintings would have been supervised by the legendary I Gdé Modara, the most important painter at the court of Klungkung during this period.

The Dewa Agung Gusti Sideman ruled until 1775; he was succeeded by his son, then by his grandson, and his line of descendants continued to reign until the beginning of the twentieth century. At the time when the ominous shadow of Dutch colonial power began to spread from Batavia across to Bali, Klungkung was ruled by the Dewa Agung Semarabhawa.

The kingdoms of Badung and Tabanan in southern Bali fell to the Dutch in 1906. On April 17, 1908, the Dutch attacked Klungkung, and fire broke out in the royal compound. To this day it is rumored the fire was started not by the Dutch but by the local people, who seized the opportunity of the confused state of affairs to rebel against the *raja.* Like the royal courts of Badung and Tabanan earlier, the Dewa Agung and his large

retinue of family, followers and retainers marched to their death in the face of the advancing Dutch army. The gold and silver decorations and beautifully colored ceremonial costumes of the royal procession glittered in the sun. In Bali, this form of collective suicide, expressing pride, dignity and royal majesty, is referred to as *puputan,* "a fight to the end."

By April 28, 1908, the Dutch had seized control of Klungkung, the last Balinese kingdom to fall. As far as can be ascertained, the only buildings of the royal compound to survive the fire were the *bale* of Kertha Gosa, the *bale* Kambang, the main gate of the palace and the *kulkul* tower. After the Dutch ordered the demolition of the palace ruins, these few buildings were preserved and restored, along with the Taman Gili, the sacred garden with moats. On the site of the palace itself the Dutch built several small structures that appear to have been used as prisons—in convenient proximity to the Kertha Gosa pavilion, which the Dutch turned into a full-fledged Western court of justice.

In spite of this disastrous turn of events, the Balinese kings and their successors still exercised considerable influence over their people. The Dutch allowed them to continue to rule, although on a less grandiose scale than before and with many of their former powers curtailed. The Dutch, in fact, did not install a full-scale government of their own in Bali, but were represented by only two officials: the Resident, based in the northern commercial port of Singaraja, and the Controller, who lived in Badung. Moreover, although the Dutch did install a court of justice in every major town of the island, they did not interfere dramatically with Balinese customs and ways of life.

In 1909, the *bale* of Kertha Gosa became the official court of justice for the region of Klungkung. According to I Dewa Nyoman Pater, the only surviving member of the Kertha Gosa tribunal, the court was presided over by the *kerthas* (now two in number), who still acted as supreme judges. But now, in addition, the tribunal included a Dutch representative, as well as two administrators (one of them being Nyoman Pater) responsible for keeping written records of each trial. The heir to the title of Dewa Agung—who had moved with the surviving members of his family to new quarters in the western part of Klungkung—was still called upon to participate in the most important cases.

Because of the presence of the Dutch representative, unaccustomed to sitting on a mat on the ground, Western-style furniture was installed at Kertha Gosa: an intricately carved rectangular wooden table and six matching upright chairs. When the *raja* was present, he occupied the seat bearing the symbolic lion's head; the chairs with the sacred cow-head symbols were reserved for the *brahmana* judges; the Dutch representative and the administrators sat in chairs decorated with dragon-head symbols. This furniture still stands in its place in the center of the pavilion.

I Dewa Nyoman Pater recalled how unique the court of justice of Klungkung had been. The celebrated ceiling contributed greatly to that uniqueness, since the paintings of *Bhima Swarga* played a significant role in the administration of justice, looming overhead to be consulted by the judges much as one would consult a text of law.

Those who had broken the law, and who therefore had to be tried, were now obliged to attend their own trial. Their relatives were made to wait in the *bale* Kambang. The accused, kneeling before the mighty tribunal, could not avoid the sight of the dreadful punishments depicted on the ceiling. But if he raised his eyes beyond, just a little above the horrors of Hell to the panels of Heaven, he could perhaps find some solace.

Because of the location of Kertha Gosa, on a corner near the busiest intersection of town, the populace of Klungkung could easily catch a glimpse of a trial from the streets below and could also have a fairly clear view of the ceiling paintings.

We do not know anything about the extent of the damages suffered by Kertha Gosa in the 1908 fire that destroyed most of the palace compound, nor—if there were then any paintings on the ceiling—whether they were completely ruined and replaced by new ones. In 1919, two years after an earthquake had devastated the entire region of Klungkung, another renovation seems to have taken place, also under the sponsorship of the Dutch. Again we have no records to give any clue about the nature of the damages.

The first known record of the ceiling paintings comes to us from a photograph, probably dating between 1930 and 1937, made by the celebrated German painter and musician Walter Spies. From this photograph it is evident that the theme of *Bhima Swarga* was depicted, but the paintings visible in it seem less elaborate than those

The kings of Bali in a rare photograph taken in the 1930s. The Raja of Klungkung is the first from left.

existing today. We know that in 1930 a great master from Kamasan, Pan Seken, directed major work on the *Bhima Swarga* paintings. Under his supervision, the project was carried out by a group of painters from Kamasan, including I Nyoman Laya, I Wayang Ngales, I Wayang Rambung, I Wayang Sempreg and I Nyoman Dogol. It was probably after the completion of this work that Walter Spies took his photograph; unfortunately, his picture is incomplete and shows only vaguely the eastern face of the ceiling and part of the northern segment. From the photograph, it would appear either that the paintings had been done directly on the wood of the ceiling or that painted wooden panels had been attached to the ceiling.

The latest renovation occurred in 1960, after the Dutch left Bali and Indonesia became independent. We have more precise information concerning this phase from Pan Semaris (son of Pan Seken), the painter who directed the work. Apparently, the entire ceiling was replaced in 1960, and new paintings were made, still depicting the story of *Bhima Swarga* but adding a great deal of detail. This time the paintings were executed on asbestos plates. Pan Semaris and his team took six months to complete the project. We do not know who sponsored this work, since neither the Klungkung municipal office nor the Bali Museum in Denpasar has any records of the 1960 renovation.

In 1982 eight panels were replaced, but the quality of the new paintings is sadly inferior—especially the colors, due to the use of acrylic paints.[14] The seasonal monsoon rains and the hot, humid climate cause rapid deterioration of the paintings and have, in fact, already begun to take their toll on the 1960 renovation.

The Balinese have always accepted the deterioration of art as an unquestioned fact of life. Artists and craftsmen create things of great beauty, not with an eye to posterity or permanence, but only with the intention that they should serve whatever special function is assigned them. Again, as long as tradition and religious belief are alive, the various crafts are alive as well; the Balinese serenely view the decay of a work of art as a natural process. When it has almost been destroyed, they replace it with a new work. Within this frame of reference, then, the Balinese can have little or no concept of restoration as such, but only of replacement. And in replacing a work of art, they always modify it—sometimes slightly, sometimes drastically. In the case of Kertha Gosa, although

A photograph of Kertha Gosa believed to have been taken by Walter Spies. The carved furniture still stands in its original place.

View of Kertha Gosa and surrounding ponds.

*This is not merely a wish to preserve a very special series of paintings, but also undoubtedly a response to the many museum-minded visitors who "collect" and preserve works of art.

unused historical monument it is today.

Until 1982, any visitor could enter Kertha Gosa unhindered, but now one must pay an entrance fee. The pavilion floor is surrounded by a wooden fence, so that visitors cannot go to the very center to look up at the ceiling paintings but can see them only from along the sides. Such pragmatic changes indicate that the people of Klungkung have begun to realize the uniqueness of Kertha Gosa, particularly the beauty of the 1960 renovation, in which no artificial dyes were used. They are now taking measures to preserve the building as carefully as possible.* Embodying as it does nearly every aspect of Balinese civilization—visual arts, literature, law, architecture, religious and philosophical belief, history—Kertha Gosa is, in fact, the most exquisite and complete example of Balinese art and culture. And most fascinating of all is its painted ceiling; in symbolically depicting the afterlife, this ceiling mirrors, on a multitude of levels, the Balinese view of the *present* life here on earth.

Balinese Traditional Painting

The ceiling of Kertha Gosa is painted in a traditional Balinese manner that conforms to a style called *wayang,* literally meaning "shadow figure." So closely do the shape and style of the painted figures resemble those of the carved-leather puppets of the *wayang kulit* (shadow-puppet theater) that if you were to cut a figure out of its painted background, you would have a facsimile of a shadow-play puppet in your hand. Paintings in the *wayang* style are related so intimately to shadow-theater art, both in terms of subject matter (namely, local interpretations of the *Mahabharata* and *Ramayana* stories) and in basic aesthetic qualities, that one has the impression that these paintings come to life on the stage or, conversely, that the shadow-puppets on the stage become frozen in the paintings.

The shadow theater of Bali, like many other Balinese art forms, originated in Java and was gradually incorpo-

the fundamental plot of *Bhima Swarga* seems to have remained constant throughout the renovations we know of, and although the iconography of the paintings is also a constant following strictly prescribed rules, certain visual details have been either omitted or further emphasized. In 1960 the panels were enlarged, the scenes of punishment in Hell were delineated more clearly, some scenes of punishments were added or replaced by others and paintings of the tree motif increased noticeably. In view of such continual alterations, no one can predict what the future may hold for Kertha Gosa.

The Kertha Gosa of Klungkung was used until the Dutch departed and Bali became part of the Independent Republic of Indonesia in 1950. Then the court of justice was transferred to a new location, for reasons that sound too simple for foreigners to believe but are perfectly comprehensible to the Balinese: the high pavilion of Kertha Gosa was too windy. In spite of this beautifully painted ceiling, the tribunal was moved to indoor premises as soon as they became available, thereby making Kertha Gosa the rated into Balinese culture during the period between the eleventh and fourteenth centuries. To this day, in Java, just as in Bali, it is one of the most popular forms of traditional dramatic expression, and its sociopolitical impact is still as powerful as it was centuries ago.

The center of *wayang* painting is Kamasan, a village two miles south of Klungkung, near Gelgel; therefore *wayang* is alternately referred to as the "Kamasan" style. The formal link between Kamasan and the *wayang* style of painting developed in about the sixteenth century during the reign of Dewa Agung Renggong, whose magnificent court at Gelgel associated him with Bali's "golden age." Since that era, generations of Kamasan painters have perpetuated *wayang* painting, preserving it so faithfully that it continues today to reflect Bali's Hindu-Javanese heritage in its traditional iconography and content.

Until the early twentieth century, the *wayang* style was Bali's only form of pictorial expression. The "modern" Ubud style of painting, deriving its name from the central hilly region where it arose, developed only after the arrival of the Dutch. In both content and technique, it has little in common with the traditional style of Kamasan. Whereas the *wayang* style is concerned only with the thematic material of old Javanese and Javano-Balinese literature as contained in *lontar* texts, the style of Ubud tends to represent aspects and scenes of everyday life in Bali. Walter Spies and the Dutch artist Rudolph Bonnet, who settled in Bali in the thirties, are credited with development of the more individualistic style of contemporary Balinese painting. Today the traditional and the modern schools coexist and thrive.

Although modern Balinese paintings are usually produced intentionally for their commercial appeal, the Kamasan *wayang* painters, while not unaware of the financial benefits, are still concerned with the inner spiritual life that both inspires and is inspired by their art and with preserving the paintings' integral function in the context of communal ceremonies and rituals.

In the past, when Kamasan paintings were produced on bark paper, they were displayed only on important occasions such as a temple festival, a tooth-filing ceremony,[15] a wedding or a cremation. Afterward, the paintings would normally be taken down and safely stored until another ritual called for their exhibition. (Even today, this custom is frequently observed.) In Bali's royal palaces, however, Kamasan paintings would often remain a permanent part of the decor. Today, *wayang* paintings are executed not on bark but on handwoven cotton or machine-made cloth and, occasionally, on wood or canvas panels.

In viewing a traditional Balinese painting, one must bear in mind that, in order to be understood, it should be observed not simply as visual art but as a work of literature. All *wayang* paintings are essentially "poetic adventures" depicted visually. It is from this perspective that one should approach the *Bhima Swarga* paintings of Kertha Gosa. The panels must be examined closely and each image deciphered. Like a single frame or a group of frames within a complete filmstrip, or like the popular Western comic strips, each scene of *Bhima Swarga* constitutes an essential part of the whole narrative. It is a sine qua non for the viewer-reader to be familiar with the stylistic and iconographic "vocabulary" in order to be able to recognize the different characters or situations in the story.

The overriding rule of the Kamasan school is to cover every inch of surface with design. Since the gods of Bali are believed to take delight in opulence, decorations must be rich and colorful, indicating that man has offered his utmost in terms of artistic effort. One might say that the Balinese gods have a horror vacui; they are not pleased by an artistic gift that is scanty or stingy or that appears to have been done hastily and without proper dedication. The painter must fill the background with a variety of motifs reminiscent of the traditional Javanese batik's complex patterns: clouds representing the atmosphere, short wavy lines imitating heat haze, birds in flight, butterflies, flames, bushes, rocks.

The artists divide each scene or episode from the

Balinese contemporary Ubud painting. Here, the artist makes "tourism" the subject of his art.

next either by inserting vertical ornamentation or by placing adjacent figures in two contiguous scenes back to back. In the Kamasan school, various vertical ornamentations are employed, and one can find each of these decorative motifs in the Kertha Gosa paintings. Among the most frequently used are the wall motif, imitating the walls of Balinese temples, and an ornament that resembles a fighting cock's colorful comb; sometimes a sharp triangular rocklike pattern supporting the comb is added to this. All these ornaments run vertically, usually along the entire length of a panel, thus creating a genuine effect of separation.

In all Kamasan paintings, an extremely important leitmotif is the tree. Almost every scene in Hell is dominated by a massive tree, which serves to separate each punishment from the next. Trees also evoke the idyllic atmosphere of Heaven, where pairs of trees create a sense of balance and harmony. Spiral creepers wind around some tree trunks, while others are completely bare, with their branches ending in the colorful foliage of meticulously drawn triangular leaves joined in triads. Reminiscent of the sacred *waringin* (or banyan) trees found in every Balinese village, these decorative trees infuse the panels with an aura of sanctity.

Iconography

When we examine the most significant part of the paintings—the characters themselves—we find extraordinary iconographic wealth. The social status and personality of each character are revealed in the paintings by a variety of subtle and highly precise details. In general, such stylistic features as costume, hair style, headdress and jewelry indicate social rank, whereas certain specific facial and bodily characteristics suggest the individual's nature—for instance, whether refined (*alus*) or coarse (*kasar*). A demon, for example, who by definition is *kasar,* may simultaneously be a king; therefore, while his physical attributes will indicate his coarse nature, he will be clothed in the same manner as a king of more refined nature.

In iconographic language, color performs an important function. Ocher or very light brown is used for painting the flesh of the gods and the noble *alus* figures, whereas *kasar* characters can be recognized immediately by their brownish-red flesh.

The angle of the head and the body attitude are also significant. While the bodies of humans and gods appear in full frontal position, their heads are always drawn from a three-quarter perspective. Demons (*raksasa*) are represented somewhere in between, with eyes and nose at a three-quarter angle but the mouth in profile. Animals are always painted in profile.

A refined *alus* figure can be recognized by an eye elongated in the shape of a fish or a lotus petal. Interestingly enough, in the case of a refined male, a straight line runs under the eye; the opposite is evidenced for a refined female, whose eye is delineated by a straight line running across the top, creating an effect of demure shyness—considered a sign of grace and femininity.

In a refined figure, the eyebrows form an elegant arch, like an Indian bow; whereas unrefined figures have eyebrows meeting at the bridge of the nose, where they are separated by two small lines symbolizing wrinkles of coarse skin, such as are seen in someone like a farmer who

Bhima

has been exposed to too much sun. Demons are painted with eyebrows ending in two fangs just above the nose.

Except for our central figure Bhima, refined males are normally clean shaven. Coarse characters, on the other hand, are often depicted with tufts of hair sprouting from the sides of their face. Animals and demons are also quite hairy.

Noses differ radically: thin and straight, with a mere suggestion of nostrils on a refined face; or large and round, with distinct nostrils, on an unrefined face.

The lips of a refined individual must be thin and gracefully shaped, showing a glimpse of white, uniform teeth. Coarse characters and animals are portrayed with oversize mouths and pointed teeth, symbolizing their aggressive nature. Demons' mouths are truly ghastly, with sharply pointed teeth and monstrous fangs.

Only refined males and females are endowed with delicate hands and slender fingers, slightly arched at the end of long and elegant arms. The gesture of the hand (*mudra*) is highly significant, forming a vital aspect of all Balinese figurative art, particularly in the Balinese dance. A vast range of emotional states is indicated primarily by means of the *mudra*. In this rich and highly complex vocabulary of gestures, the curve of a finger, the turn of a wrist, the position of a hand can communicate sadness, anger, devotion, shyness, love, authority or nearly any other feeling imaginable.

In the paintings, the right hand is almost always active, while the left hand remains motionless. This visual convention conforms to the strict Balinese code of etiquette. It is the right hand that expresses emotions, touches food and accepts gifts, since the right hand is considered "clean"; whereas the left hand, used mainly to wash one's body, is taboo, "unclean," and must never be used in any social or, above all, sacred activity.

All the noble characters and the gods wear ornaments, usually bracelets and bangles on the upper arms and around the ankles. In the earlier period, these ornaments were often painted with gold leaf (*prada*), an expensive and elaborate process. Today such jewelry is painted yellow, simulating the original gold. The refined nature of the nobles and gods is expressed with appropriate elegance in their costumes, too: fabrics are richly decorated with flowery patterns, and garments resemble those worn by Balinese dancers in the roles of warrior, king and princess.

In the paintings, social standing can also be indicated by the hierarchical position of the characters, the size of their body, the side on which they are placed (that is, on the right or the left side of the scene). For example, in the *Bhima Swarga* story the stature of Siwa, Heaven's most prominent god, is far larger and more imposing than that of any other god, and Bhima overpowers all other humans in the narrative. His servants Twalen and Mredah usually appear side by side, with Mredah, Twalen's son, placed slightly below his father. Age and social status are similarly indicated in all the representations of the five Pandawa brothers, with Nakula and Sahadewa, the youngest, standing behind Arjuna, the third in line.

The Characters

The major characters of the story are easy to recognize because of the special attributes associated with them. It is noteworthy that in the case of the hero, Bhima, we find a rare departure from the highly stylized type dictated by convention—a departure that clearly singles him out as an individual. A number of iconographic peculiarities emphasize his uniqueness: whereas all his brothers wear richly decorated epaulettes on their shoulders, he does not. Since his power is strictly physical, his body must be unhampered, ready to rush into battle. Wrapped around his body like an elegant ribbon is a flowing *sarong* of a special black-and-white checked material (*kain poleng*) that in Bali is believed to possess magic protective qualities.[16] Unlike other noble characters, Bhima has a mustache, denoting his virility and formidable physical strength. His aggressive, quarrelsome personality is indicated by an unusually round face and by skin slightly darker than that of his brothers; and his impulsiveness and courage are symbolized in his round pupils and in his eyes, which, unlike those of other refined figures, are circular. Although slender-waisted, he takes an aggressive stance, with legs spread wide in the *malpal* position assumed by the famous Balinese *baris* (warrior dancer) as he executes his leaps—knees raised and ankles bent so that his feet touch the ground at an angle. His importance as a warrior is further emphasized by the position allotted him in all battle scenes: he always appears in the center of the panels, whether fighting among demons or gods—literally at the center of the action. All the events revolve around him.

One of Bhima's most important features—again an attribute assigned to him alone—is his right thumb, which ends in a very long curved nail protruding from a closed fist, a sign of magical potency. Finally, he wields a weapon belonging to no one else, his famous bejeweled club. The only personal feature that is not unique is his hair: it is like that of all the other Pandawa brothers (except Yudhisthira), arranged in an elaborate style shaped like a lobster claw rising from the back of the head.

Twalen and Mredah, his retainers, appear in the paintings almost as often as Bhima; they represent, as it were, his "alter ego," the superhuman hero's reflection on the ordinary human plane. The two clowns resemble each other closely and can be distinguished mainly by size— Twalen is larger than his son—and by costume. By virtue of their association with Bhima, they partake of his magical power, and their dress reflects this: Twalen is clad in a *sarong* of the same black-and-white checked *kain poleng* that Bhima wears (although his *sarong* is knotted around him clumsily like that of a farmer, rather than flowing elegantly like Bhima's); Mredah's *sarong* is red-and-white checked, signifying a magical quality of less potency. In addition, Twalen is more potbellied than his son. Aside from these differences, Mredah appears as merely a miniature version of Twalen, truly dwarflike, and the two always appear together except in battle scenes, where they sometimes lose sight of each other. They

resemble semihuman monkeys—hairy, with large, knobby chins. Each wears his hair atop his head in a small ponytail. Curiously enough, although they are depicted with eyes in the shape of puffy fish, normally associated with members of the peasant *sudra* class, their teeth are fine and uniform, a sign of special refinement. This anomaly points out the very essence of the clowns' personality and role in the story: their utterly serious devotion to Bhima and at the same time their comic nature—a delightful admixture of the sublime and the ridiculous that makes them a Balinese version of the "wise fool." Like Bhima's club, Twalen's weapon is a symbol of power. But it is a comic symbol, a distortion of Bhima's weapon, for it is pear-shaped at the tip and is recognized by the Balinese as a phallic symbol. In the shadow plays, the *dalang* always draws a roar of laughter from the audience by turning the weapon about to show the phallic butt. Normally, Twalen's weapon travels across the *wayang kulit* screen with a slow, wavy, ponderous motion, in

Twalen

Mredah

Kunti

Legong dancer

obvious contrast to the swift action of Bhima's club.

Queen Kunti, Bhima's mother, can be easily recognized in the paintings by her white hair arranged in the turbanlike style called *ketu,* which is also generally worn by *brahmana* priests and by some of the gods portrayed by the Kamasan school. Her regal nature is reflected in her apparel, a batik *sarong* with rich flowery motifs and a cloth corset wrapped tightly around her breast—a costume similar to that of the Balinese *legong* dancers.

Yudhisthira, the eldest Pandawa prince, wears his hair in a style uniquely his, tied at the back in a low, folded ponytail. His *sarong* is wrapped around him in the elaborate ceremonial style of royal males. He is bare-chested and wears richly decorated epaulettes on his shoulders, for his power is psychological and intellectual, so that his body need not be free to move swiftly like that of Bhima.

Yama, the deity of Hell, is painted with demonic fea-tures magnified to the extreme. He epitomizes the *kasar* nature. He has teeth on his cheeks and forehead and huge tusklike teeth protruding from his enormous mouth; his skin is covered with blotches. He rides a monstrous animal, half-tiger, half-elephant, or an enormous buffalo with a flaming tail. He is armed with a mace. At the same time, he wears a crown and is surrounded by the divine yellow halo, for he is a god and a king as well as a demon.

Yama's minister, Jogormanik, is an extremely popular character in Bali. When his shadow appears on the *wayang kulit* screen, there is always a roar from the audience, for he is indeed imposing—an enormous figure with a huge belly and skin blotched with distinctive stains. Except for three wedge-shaped tufts of black hair, he is completely bald. He often appears in the company of Delem and Sangut, the servants of the "left" side of the conflict; they perform on the "left side" what Twalen and Mredah perform on the "right." Not father and son but brothers, these characters are not essentially "evil." They are simply the counterparts of Twalen and Mredah, possessing many of the same attributes as the Pandawa clown servants and, similarly, enjoying great popularity among the Balinese. They resemble deformed, almost emaciated monkeys, with tiny legs and enormous mouths. Delem is coarser than Sangut.

Siwa, the chief god in Heaven, stands out with his imposing stature. His white skin represents unquestioned nobility. As the deity who holds together the four corners of the world, he is the only god with four arms. Moreover, he has a third eye—the eye of wisdom—in the middle of the forehead. With one of his two right hands, he holds the chalice containing the water of immortality. Behind him stand his attendants. He is enveloped by the golden-yellow halo that is the attribute of all the gods, symbolizing magical power, luminosity and immortality.

The next important god is Bayu, Bhima's spiritual father and god of the wind. He resembles Bhima in almost every respect, except that he does not have Bhima's long curved thumbnail or bejeweled weapon. And unlike that of his mortal son, the yellow halo surrounds his body.

Finally, we encounter Sanghyang Acintya, the only god represented with body and face in full frontal position. The highest deity, even surpassing Siwa, Acintya appears twice at Kertha Gosa: once in the scene where he resurrects Bhima, and the second time in the very last panel of Heaven. Separated from all the other gods, in both scenes he stands alone in the *yoga* position, with his right leg bent and arched and his palms pressed together. A yellow background painted behind him and an unusually luminous halo endow his white body with an ethereal quality. In the *wayang kulit* performance, his figure is as important as that of the cosmic tree (*kakayonan*) as a motif of divine protective power; it appears on the screen together with the tree at the beginning and at the end of every shadow play.

The paintings depicting Hell differ considerably in size and in detail from the ones of Heaven. In general, the figures in Hell are much larger and the panels less busy and opulent than those of Heaven. Rather incongruously, birds and butterflies float serenely overhead, oblivious to the gruesome activities below. Unfolding on a rocky terrain representing the ruggedness of the earth, Hell's battle scenes are mobbed, fiery—a confusion of blood-spattered bodies, legs, arms and weapons. Arrows bend and break as they approach their target to show the power (*sakti*) of Bhima and his retainers.

In Heaven, however, battle scenes are not bloody. Bhima as usual occupies the center of the war panels, but his body is much smaller than in Hell; this is probably due to the stylistic principle of hierarchy, since Bhima's importance diminishes somewhat when he is among the gods. Rather than the throngs of broken arrows filling the spaces in Hell's battle scenes, flames of radiating magic fill the space around the warrior Bhima in Heaven. The gods, though armed and evidently battling against him, are portrayed not as attacking him directly, but rather as being somewhat removed from him. This imagery would suggest that war in Heaven is more a psychological or spiritual, rather than physical, confrontation.

Unlike the paintings of Hell, those of Heaven are filled with minute, almost indecipherable details. The blessed souls, the gods' attendants and the gods themselves are all tightly packed in a hierarchical arrangement. The deities' palaces bear close resemblance to the sacred shrines called *meru* in Bali. Vertically arranged, of uneven number and decreasing in size from bottom to top, pagoda-style, the roofs of these shrines are dark brown, almost black, and are composed of rolled sugar-palm fibers and several layers of fibrous material.

These paintings of Heaven reflect the highest degree of elegance and richness, that very luxuriant atmosphere in which the gods of Bali are believed to take such delight. Ultimately, these lush scenes are the epitome of the horror vacui of Balinese traditional painting.

When I first saw the Kertha Gosa ceiling, I could not help feeling overwhelmed by the visual richness of this display. That very first encounter marked the point of departure for my fascinating adventure. I looked up at Heaven, and then slightly lower at Hell, my eyes drawn to the individual panels of *Bhima Swarga*. It was this enduring story, its universal message, that I had to, in the end, find and tell.

Soon I found out that all the Balinese I encountered knew the story of *Bhima Swarga* as intimately as the average Westerner knows the tales of Cinderella and Snow White. But even though the main story line of Bhima's journey remained constant, nearly everyone recounted his own, slightly modified version of it, letting the imagination run free, inventing different incidents and dreaming up new details to embellish the plot. I found this particularly true for the various punishments to which errant souls were condemned.

It is, of course, precisely this marvelous freedom of the imagination, this unrepressed power of mythmaking, the merging of dream with reality, this love of storytelling for no reason other than the sheer pleasure of storytelling, that enriches and sustains the vitality of an oral tradition. In Bali, as in other traditional societies, the oral transmission of mythic or quasi-historical epics and legends is so deeply rooted in the culture that it is impossible to trace

The figures of Bhima, Twalen and Mredah on their way to Swarga in the paintings of Kertha Gosa.

the origins of a particular story. It goes back, one might say, to the culture's own "unconscious." A living oral tradition serves the important function of sharpening a community's sense of identity and continuity and, at the same time, of reinforcing in each member of the community that vital feeling of belonging.

It was precisely the mysteries of this living oral tradition, with all its ambiguous and elusive qualities, that had always fascinated me.

With the assistance of Ida Bagus Ngurah's enthusiastic Balinese friends, I recorded the *dalang* performance one May night of the full moon. Later, with the help of other friends those tapes were transcribed and translated.

Although I have taken some pains to reproduce as

closely as possible the various "voices" of the different characters, the text I present here is by no means a literal translation. Whenever Kawi is employed in the original, as for the gods and the noble characters, I have translated their speech into a more formal English. With Bhima, I have deliberately chosen not to make his English "poetic," for although he employs Kawi, he is by his very nature a man of action, and his particular type of Kawi bears the imprint of his personality. It is highly proper and noble, but also imperious and commanding. Rather than embroidering his sentences with flowery formalisms, adverbs or adjectives, he speaks quite abruptly and directly to the point; he has no time for poetry.

Twalen and Mredah, the clowns, speak vernacular

29

Balinese, far less elegant than Kawi. But even in their language, one observes a marked difference between the way they address their superiors and the way they talk to each other. In my text I have tried to convey these two styles of speech, employing simple but polite English in the first case and, in the second, the rougher, often quite coarse and crude language they use with each other. I have not "invented," but have provided the closest possible English equivalent of the original Balinese "slang."

The main part of this book is the text of *Bhima Swarga,* as "translated" from the *dalang's* narration and based on the painted panels of the Kertha Gosa ceiling. Each illustration presents a photographic reproduction of an individual painted panel. On the printed page opposite, I provide the portion of the text pertaining to that particular panel or panels. For certain scenes, the *dalang* narrated at great length; for others, only a few words were spoken.

If the reader will use his imagination to interpolate the music, the voices, the movement that I have not been able to capture in words, if we can hear the *dalang's* many different voices and the fugue of the musical accompaniment, if we can watch the static painted images transform themselves into animated puppets casting their shadows upon the screen . . . if we can lift the printed words and images off the pages of this book and conjure up theater, we will be able, in some way, to experience the spectacle that I was so fortunate to witness on that Balinese night of the full moon—that very singular experience at a time and in a place with a profound work of art.

If this experience comes alive for the reader in some small way, it is the best tribute I could pay to the legend and life of the *Bhima Swarga* of Kertha Gosa, to the Balinese people themselves and to the mystery of "the story."

❖

BHIMA SWARGA

ONCE THERE LIVED a great king named Pandu. He reigned with majesty as the head of the Pandawa dynasty, and his two wives, Kunti and Madri, were renowned for their beauty. Now it happened that one day, as Pandu was strolling through the forest, he came upon two deer making love. Being a passionate hunter, he could not resist this tempting target. He drew his bow and shot so skillfully that both animals were struck by a single arrow. But, to his astonishment, as soon as the arrow had pierced their hearts, the two deer vanished and in their place lay a man and a woman. The wounded man shrieked at the king, "Damn you! How dare you commit such a cruel act? I am a priest, and my wife and I assumed the form of deer so that we could enjoy each other in peace." As he lay dying, the priest gasped with his last breath, "You will not escape punishment for this, heartless archer! Henceforth, if ever you engage in lovemaking, you, like us, will be struck dead. Thus do I swear this curse upon your head!"

Horrified, Pandu returned home and told his wives of the disaster that had befallen him. He had no choice: from that moment on, he was obliged to observe a life of absolute chastity. Naturally this news came as a terrible blow to both women. Whereas Madri, Pandu's second wife, was miserable at the thought of spending the rest of her life in complete abstinence, Kunti, the first wife, had an advantage that made her sorrow somewhat easier to bear. As a young girl, she had been granted a special gift: the power to summon any god she desired for lovemaking—a power, however, that could be used only five times.

Kunti knew that the spell worked, because before her marriage to Pandu she had once been overcome by uncontrollable curiosity about whether the power was indeed genuine. To test it, she had called upon the sun-god Surya, and he had appeared instantly, giving her a son without damaging her virginity. To protect her reputation from malicious gossip, she was obliged to keep the affair secret and thus left the infant on the bank of the Yamuna River. The baby had been found and adopted by a chariot driver. This child, called Karna, later became a sworn enemy of the Pandawas.

Now, at last, Kunti had a perfect excuse to use the charm again. First she summoned Dharma, god of virtue, and in due time she gave birth to Yudhisthira. Next she chose Bayu, god of the wind, with whom she conceived Bhima. When her amorous passion again grew intense, she used her gift for the fourth time to call upon Indra, god of thunder and rain. Nine months later the handsome Arjuna was born.

Meanwhile Madri, who had not been endowed with the blissful powers of Kunti, grew jealous. In a moment of great distress she begged Kunti to let her use the charm for the fifth and final time. Kunti, realizing how selfish she had been, agreed to Madri's request.

Madri pondered for a long time about how she could best make use of this one and only opportunity. She finally hit upon the clever idea of summoning the twin gods, the Aswins, so that her pleasure in lovemaking would be doubled. From that memorable union, the twins Nakula and Sahadewa were born.

It was said that this ingenious act of Madri's greatly upset Kunti, who wished that she herself had thought of invoking the twin gods. But as time passed, the two queens came to live in harmony, for, after all, they had both had their share of wishes come true, as well as the joy of bearing children.

Thus, all went well in the royal palace, and the king and his wives were filled with contentment as they watched their five sons grow into fine, strong young men. But late one afternoon, disaster struck. King Pandu, moved to intense passion by the extraordinary colors of the sunset, was overcome by Madri's beauty, and, filled with irresistible desire, he made love to her. The dying priest's curse immediately took effect: Pandu fell dead. Then, in an agony of remorse at being partly responsible for this tragedy, Madri killed herself so that her beloved husband would not be alone in death.

The story of Bhima Swarga begins a few years later. . . .

QUEEN KUNTI, the lovely wife of the departed King Pandu, awoke one night trembling with distress. Afraid of being trapped in another terrible nightmare, she did not go back to sleep but awaited dawn in the silence of her palace.

When the first light of the new day entered her bedroom, she got up and dressed in her most regal attire. Exhausted from a thousand thoughts and shaking with anxiety, she dragged herself to the throne room. There she summoned her sons and stepsons to her presence.

First to arrive was Yudhisthira, the eldest and wisest of her sons. As he stood beside his mother, the devoted court-clowns, Twalen and Mredah, immediately followed to join him near the queen. Next came Bhima, the second son, a proud hero who bowed to no one. Soon after, the agile and handsome Arjuna arrived. Finally, the twins Nakula and Sahadewa, born to Pandu's second wife, Madri, took their place behind Bhima and Arjuna.

Yudhisthira was the first to speak: "Mother, my Lady, I beg you to explain what ails you. We are apprehensive and mystified. From your expression, it is clear that something must be terribly wrong. Your face resembles a lotus in an empty pond, faded and sad." As Yudhisthira bowed and paid his respects, Kunti answered, "It is just too much . . . oh, my children. . . ." Her sadness welled up, and sobs prevented her from speaking.

Little Mredah, the clown, broke in and said, "There is no way Her Majesty can hold back her tears. She's completely overcome with sorrow. We've gathered here to be at her service, body and soul, to do whatever must be done."

"There is a reason for my tears," said Kunti. "Last night I had just fallen asleep when a strange feeling came over me. I saw your father Pandu walking toward me, accompanied by Dewi Madri. They had come from the land of the dead, and their faces were contorted with all the sufferings of Hell."

The queen went on to describe in detail the pained expressions of Pandu and Madri. As she spoke, a grave silence descended on her listeners and hung like a heavy black cloud over their heads.

"What can we do for them?" Kunti finally cried out. "If you cannot think of any way to relieve your parents of their misery, I will have to join them. Knowing they are in Hell, I can no longer live in peace on this earth."

At first no one was able to cast off the oppressive cloud of silence. Then Bhima sprang up in anger.

"Since when are the Pandawas speechless? Our mother has begged for help." His heart was pounding with sorrow. Looking straight into his mother's eyes, he declared fiercely, "I will not be long. If, as you say, our parents are in Hell, I will release them. Neither god nor goddess will stand in my way."

At once, Bhima's journey was announced, and palace messengers were sent to all parts of the kingdom. Elaborate ceremonies were performed under the full moon. It is said that for days before the prince's departure, the brilliance of the sun and the moon was obscured by clouds of incense rising to the gods of Swarga.

The palace was abuzz with preparations. The sounds of music and dance, shadow plays and chanting, filled its halls. Charged with excitement, everyone—the queen, the princes, the courtiers and all the people—forgot their fatigue and lost all desire to sleep.

Only the clowns Twalen and Mredah were worried. They hid behind the monumental offerings in the royal temple or among the crowds of children. If they remained unseen, they thought, they would soon be forgotten. Ah, wishful thinking! More than once they were caught and sent to help the others.

Twalen and Mredah both knew, only too well, that when Bhima started on his journey they would have to accompany him. Orders were orders. That was their reward for being faithful and reliable. The clowns were to the Pandawa family just as a dog is to its master, or as the talking gecko is to every house.

The night before Bhima's departure was a special night. Their eyes closed, the court musicians played continuously. Despite the great crowd that filled every corner of the throne room, the ceremony of departure was an intimate and moving family affair.

Bhima—not the queen—occupied the seat of honor. With his chest bared, the signs of his incredible strength were evident. He gazed into the distance, losing himself somewhere far beyond the palace walls. Twalen and Mredah, appearing from behind the throne, trembled with apprehension, as they always did in unusual and unpredictable situations. The very music itself vibrated with nervous expectation, filling the air with high-pitched sounds. Queen Kunti stood to one side, encircled by Yudhisthira, Arjuna and the twins.

Suddenly, before anyone could grasp what was going on, something extraordinary happened to Bhima: Kunti's spirit entered his heart, Yudhisthira's power of thought penetrated his mind, Nakula and Sahadewa's ability to solve problems and execute tasks flowed into his arms, and Arjuna's agility flooded every muscle of his body.

This all happened so swiftly and silently that no one realized the cause of the sudden change in Bhima's appearance. One witness reported that, as soon as his mother and brothers surrounded him, Bhima became so powerful that some of those who were present fell to their knees and prayed. The prince seemed to burst with the same mighty energy as the sacred volcano Gunung Agung during one of its eruptions.

But Mredah was still skeptical and kept pestering his father with questions.

"He said he won't be long . . . that he's going to bring his parents back. How? How's he going to do that? How's he going to get to Swarga?"

Twalen tried everything to calm him, but Mredah kept on. "How about us? Then what? After that, then what?"

Twalen, needless to say, was as frightened as little Mredah, but he tried to conceal it.

"Son, shut up. There's nothing to worry about. We'll come back. He said we'll come back."

Huge mounds of delectable foods were carried in and consumed. But Mredah grew more and more nervous and could not even think of eating.

"Bah, big words from your big mouth," he said to Twalen. "You! You haven't even found out what we are supposed to do."

This was too much for Twalen to bear. "OK! Hold me down and kick me in the head! My very own son—criticizing me like that. . . . That's the thanks I get for taking care of you, for feeding you every day with my own hands."

Mredah bowed his head.

"You don't know when to stop," Twalen scolded, "calling me big mouth. And to think you've been to school. What for? You're grown up, and you still don't know your place."

Mredah bent his head even lower.

"Listen," said Twalen severely, "just listen! An old man is like a bird: feed him and he'll sing; if you don't, not only will you be wrong, but he won't be strong. Treat him well, and he'll last; if not, you'll surely lose your grasp. Never, never get fresh with your father."

Several hours later, when the sun rose like a circle of flames burning in the sky, Bhima, Twalen and Mredah were already on their way to Swarga.

The prince was far ahead. His retainers could hardly keep up with him.

"Hurry up! Hurry up and stop complaining. Complaining slows people down!" Bhima shouted.

Bhima walked as if he were flying. He strode forward, casting an ever-changing shadow, never pausing at a single spot for more than an instant. Twalen and Mredah stumbled along, running clumsily behind.

"Where's Swarga, Dad?" Mredah asked.

"Seven miles south, for all I know," Twalen replied.

They chattered on about anything to stifle the fear they felt inside. Mredah even started singing a meaningless song.

"Do not waste time!" Bhima cried out. And on they went. They crossed mountains and valleys, steep cliffs and ravines, until they reached a broad river—the boundary between this world and Swarga.

"We are up against the mighty river Sarayu," Bhima announced.

"What a current! Deep and wide and swift. All that water! Pure water!" exclaimed Twalen, sinking to the ground exhausted.

"We must determine how to cross it," Bhima said with great seriousness.

"But it's so deep and wide and wet!" Twalen wailed.

"What is that?" the prince asked suddenly, pointing at a rock.

"It's a stone. I just noticed it, too—a rock," Twalen replied quickly.

Several large stones were scattered along the riverbank. The three travelers were already planning to use them to build a bridge when, suddenly, the rocks came to life and began to move.

Twalen screamed at the top of his lungs. Mredah cowered behind him.

"Let's get out of here, Bhima, sir! This place is full of crocodiles! They scare me to death—those jaws! Those fangs!" Twalen cried out.

"Twalen! Mredah!" Bhima commanded. "Do not be afraid."

"Dad . . . Ddddad . . . don't be scared . . . he was born the same way we were, the crocodile," stammered Mredah.

But Twalen, who could usually control himself, shook with fear. No crocodile had ever been recorded in *his* family registry.

"Listen to me," Bhima began solemnly. "When we were born, we were not born alone. Our spiritual tutelary brothers at birth were the Kanda Empat—that is, the amniotic fluid, the blood, the umbilical cord and the afterbirth—all of which protected our growth in the womb. This crocodile is nothing less than a manifestation of one of them."

As soon as Bhima was finished, the crocodile crawled up to him and, happy to be recognized at last, kindly offered to carry Bhima and his companions across the river.

Twalen could not believe what was happening. Mredah was speechless.

Their journey continued from one adventure to the next. Every time they encountered a dangerous beast, Bhima would invariably say, "Here is another brother. Stay close by."

When they reached a forest, Twalen was awestruck. "Oh my soul, what a jungle! Who planted all those trees? Somebody really outdid himself. Coconuts, saplings, rattan, palm trees, holy flowers . . . just like the real thing."

Everything that was needed for a cremation was growing there: the right kind of bamboo, the right kind of wood for coffins and the right kind of flowers.

All at once a mountain of red clay pots, stacked one atop the other, each one inscribed with a name, loomed before them.

"How many cremations there must have been! When it all goes up in smoke, this is where it comes—stacked up like a volcano," Twalen observed.

As they continued on their way, they caught sight of a great path, as smooth as a highway, that ran straight along the valley floor.

"Why are we hugging the side of the mountain when we could be down there marching along with ease?" Mredah asked.

Bhima, who normally spoke only when it was really necessary, answered: "That is the road of the Ninth Direction. It is forbidden to go there. It is only for the truly purified souls. We are headed in the opposite way."

But Twalen's explanation was clearer to Mredah: "If you haven't had the right cremation, according to who you are, you wouldn't last two minutes on that road. All kinds of things would get in your way. You have to have the proper send-off or you'll never make it. We're not even dead yet; we couldn't possibly get through."

"How do you know?" Mredah insisted.

"I know," Twalen replied impatiently. "And now shut up."

For a while the two royal retainers seemed to have forgotten about Hell, but Bhima knew that their journey was about to end. All of a sudden, just as Twalen and Mredah were giggling and making jokes, they stopped dead in their tracks as if struck by lightning.

Startled and pale, they cowered behind the prince, using his body as a shield. There, right below them, was Hell—yes, actually Hell itself, the notorious Yamaloka, Yama's kingdom, an awesome landscape of turmoil, smoke and infinite pain extending for miles around, a neatly ordered world of horrendous scenes. From their vantage point at the edge of the mountain, they could see it quite clearly. A steep path led down the mountainside to the entrance of Yamaloka. But before beginning their descent, Bhima stopped where they were at the cliff edge to rest awhile. After all, he had never faced Hell before, and he needed to plan his actions carefully before entering the dangerous place where King Pandu and Dewi Madri were. He was calm, but Twalen and Mredah clung to him and shivered with fear as they peered below. A vast panorama of the greatest sins and punishments of mankind unfolded before them, and they could scarcely believe what they saw. . . .

First, they spotted several souls gathered in one corner, waiting for judgment. They were conversing, probably exchanging the stories of their lives and sharing their fears about what was going to happen. But Twalen and Mredah could not hear what they were saying.

"Look at that tree!" Twalen exclaimed, pointing at a huge tree—the *kaiu curiga* tree—whose branches towered over the souls.

"Oh, my god!" moaned Mredah. "All those sharp blades hanging like leaves over their heads. Poor souls!"

It was then that Togtogsil, the one-eyed demon, appeared. Instantly, Twalen and Mredah forgot all about the tree and stared at Togtogsil as if his monstrous body were a magnet. The demon was questioning the souls of two men.

Just behind him, a pig was gnawing at the body of a man who had been a dishonest butcher, selling pork for the price of beef.

"This is the punishment given to all those who cheat others," said Twalen in a trembling voice, pretending to be a connoisseur of such matters.

Suddenly the sky of Yamaloka reddened ferociously. The flames of the Tambra Goh Muka, an enormous iron cauldron with cowhead handles, shot into the air. Bhuta Abang and one of his fellow demons were throwing sinners into the boiling waters, while Bhuta Ode Ode busied himself with the endless task of keeping the fires going eternally.

"Dad, Dad . . . what the hell have those souls done to deserve such torture?" asked Mredah, expressing himself in his usual inimitable way.

"The woman about to be thrown in was lazy beyond belief. While the man . . . well . . . the man was a real troublemaker. He caused confusion left and right, wherever he went, just for fun."

"And what about those who are already boiling?"

"They're there for corruption, my son," Twalen replied in a solemn tone.

"Co . . . what?"

"Cor-rup-tion," Twalen replied impatiently, "the most common disease of mankind."

"Ah! *E*ruption," Mredah echoed. "It must have something to do with the crater of a volcano," he thought, looking at the shape of the cauldron, and not daring to ask any more questions about the subject.

51

Just then Twalen caught sight of Suratma, the renowned record-keeper of Yamaloka. He was arguing fiercely with a *dukun,* a folk healer, who was trying to defend himself against accusations. But the demon knew the truth about him.

"How do you know he's a *dukun?*" Mredah asked.

"From the magic Ushada *lontar,* the book of medicine, he's still holding tightly in his left hand," Twalen replied. "Bad news, this doctor—too smart for his own good. Always charged too much for his services, constantly bragged and falsely advertised his success. He got away with it all his life on earth, but here he won't, I can assure you."

Next they noticed a man and a woman fleeing from the sword of the demon Wirosa, who was about to strike them for having stolen rice.

"Always remember this, son," said Twalen emphatically. "No matter how hungry you are, *never* steal rice. *Never!* Stealing rice is like stealing money. The punishment for this sin leaves no chance for mercy."

"Yes . . . yes. . . . Got the message, Dad," Mredah answered, feeling suddenly very hungry.

Then silence fell between Twalen and Mredah. It was as if they were purposely holding their breath in an effort to control the terror they felt.

"Be quiet! There's Jogormanik," Twalen whispered to his son.

"I *am* quiet," Mredah retorted. "Jogormanik, brrrr. . . . How huge he is! How dark and blotchy his skin! What fangs!"

"Shut up! For *hell's* sake, shut up!" Twalen screamed at the top of his lungs.

Meanwhile Jogormanik, the demon minister of Yamaloka, was calmly going about his business. He was not terrifying anyone but, on the contrary, was chatting amiably with a good soul who was about to leave for Heaven. However, from where they stood, Twalen and Mredah had no way of knowing this. All they had heard about Jogormanik was his reputation as the most dreaded and evil demon of Hell.

A few yards away, a man was being ferociously attacked by a huge, blotchy animal.

"An elephant?" Mredah inquired, noticing the creature's long snout reaching out like a boa constrictor to grip the neck of the man.

"That animal is many things," Twalen replied promptly. "He is an elephant with ears like a buffalo and the body of a lion. He is also the king of the jungle. Now, on behalf of all animals, he's taking revenge. The man is a hunter who killed animals left and right, just for his own pleasure."

Watching all this—in silence—was the solitary soul of a pathetic old woman.

"A woman should always get married," muttered Twalen, changing the subject altogether. "If she remains a spinster, it means something must be wrong with her character. It's a grave sin not to establish a family, not to have children. For a childless person, old age is an awful time of loneliness and sadness, and this condition naturally carries over into death. You see, whatever you are when you die is exactly what you continue to be after you're dead. Whatever you're doing and feeling at the end of life keeps right on going afterward, no change at all."

But Mredah was too young to understand the meaning of his father's words and did not pay much attention to the woman, since there was no demon lurking behind, ready to strike her.

"Son, why are you so quiet? Have you lost your tongue?" Twalen asked in astonishment.

No sooner had he said this than Mredah began to show signs of fear.

"Look, Dad! Look at what those two demons are doing to that man! They're sawing his head in half, back and forth, back and forth. . . ."

"Back and forth . . . ," Twalen echoed, changing his expression and grinning.

"Back and forth, back and forth . . . brrrr. . . . I feel it, I feel it," Mredah moaned.

"What?"

"The saw . . . my head, my head, oh what pain!" Mredah cried out, holding his head in his hands.

"That's what *you'll* get someday if you don't treat me well; you'll see. That man didn't respect his parents and grandparents, and as if that weren't bad enough, he also neglected to make offerings to his ancestors and didn't honor them with the veneration due them. He deserves every bit of that saw. Back and forth . . . back and forth."

"Dad . . . I'll always treat you well," squeaked Mredah, his voice shrill with nervousness. "Always! I promise!"

"Well, well, look who's there," Twalen interrupted, his attention already fixed on someone else.

"Who?"

"Delem and Sangut, you dummy, our very own enemies. Don't tell me you can't even recognize those little bastards anymore!"

The retainers of Yama were seated peacefully at the feet of the great Jogormanik, who was questioning two enigmatic-looking souls.

"And what have *they* done? Is it a sin to look enigmatic?" Mredah asked, puzzled and unsure of the meaning of "enigmatic," a word he had heard once and was now using for the first time in his life.

"It has nothing to do with looks," Twalen replied. "It's about the attributes of a *banci*."

"*Banci*? What's that?"

"Very simply, it means: a man who thinks and acts like a woman—effeminate, you understand? Or, a woman who thinks and acts like a man—plays soccer, for instance. It's very simple."

"Is that a sin?" Mredah asked, pretending to have completely understood the whole "simple" matter.

"No, it's not a sin; it's just something out of the ordinary. It's a kind of imperfection. And that's why a *banci*, however good his life has been, still has to spend some time in Hell before he can be admitted to the highest spheres."

A few minutes elapsed, and there was Jogormanik once again, peacefully exchanging a few words with the soul of a man.

"That man was a prince," Twalen explained. "In the family temple, he carefully guarded the *prasasti,* the book containing the history of his family. There, you see, he's holding the book in his left hand. Jogormanik is praising him for having done his duty."

"Oh, my god! Togtogsil!" Mredah cried out. "Why is he so angry? His eye is so huge!"

"Precisely," said Twalen calmly. "He's chastising a man and wife who sold their family history to a passing merchant. Togtogsil is pointing at the book and cursing them. It's a grave sin to exchange spiritual values for material wealth, to just give away your roots and traditions like that."

Not far from the dreadful scene of Togtogsil's anger, several souls were gathered under a luxuriant tree, peacefully enjoying its shade. No sooner had Twalen and Mredah begun to admire the tree's beauty when suddenly an enormous demon appeared amid its foliage.

"That's Bhu . . . Bhuta Ma . . . Maya," Twalen stammered nervously, trying to conceal his fear, "the demon of the *kaiu curiga* tree. . . ."

"The *kris* tree," Mredah gasped even more nervously than his father. At that moment, Bhuta Maya began shaking the branches so wildly that Twalen and Mredah felt the very earth under their feet shaking too, as if the very mountain on which they stood were being agitated from within. As Bhuta Maya shook the branches, hundreds of *krises* fell on the poor souls beneath and pierced their eyes.

Mredah instantly covered his eyes with his hands.

"Some say this punishment is for those who lost their minds and committed suicide. It's an unforgivable sin to end your life before its time." Twalen's voice trembled.

"Others say this punishment is for those who were sinful, not intentionally but out of ignorance," commented Mredah, as if the words did not belong to him.

"How do you know?" asked Twalen, amazed to hear his son speak so eloquently.

"I don't know," little Mredah replied, pulling his hands away from his eyes.

As soon as he peered down again, he noticed two men and a woman hanging from clumps of bamboo trees.

"Look!" he cried out to Twalen. "A mouse is gnawing at one of those ropes. It's about to snap. Just a few strands left, and then that man will fall into the flames."

"Poor people, they keep hanging on, hoping against hope," Twalen sighed. "If your children don't have children, that's what'll happen to us. Only grandchildren can liberate the souls of their grandparents. Aside from that, when old people don't have grandchildren, their life on earth becomes truly miserable. Having grandchildren is always a heavenly blessing."

Nearby, another man was chewing on one of the bamboo trees. He had entered the world of the dead with his front teeth unfiled, a symbol of demonic aggression. Behind him stood a wrathful demon raising a sword.

"He's got an eternity to chew," Mredah remarked.

"He must have learned his lesson by now," said Twalen. "Luckily we've had our teeth filed recently. If not, we'd look like him now, as horrible as those demons. People have to look their best before entering Swarga. . . ."

"There's Jogormanik again," Mredah interrupted. "My god, he seems to be everywhere."

There he was indeed, in the shade of a lovely tree. He was praising the soul of a man who had always been hospitable and generous with his guests. But on the other side of the tree, something truly dreadful was happening.

"That man," said Twalen, "used poison for revenge." At the mere mention of poison, Mredah began shaking like a leaf in the wind. "The demon is shoving a substance that itches, called *medang,* down his throat," Twalen went on. "Once it touches the tongue, not even the gods can remove it. Finally the person chokes to death. But that man can't die again and so will keep on choking and choking forever."

Mredah was so disgusted by the whole thing that he felt his tongue swell up, and almost went into convulsions.

"There's an awful witch," said Twalen, trying to take his son's mind off the idea of the poison *medang* and the infernal itching. "Just wait a minute and the demon will grab her long hair and pull it until nothing is left of her, you can bet on it."

But Mredah was so distressed that nothing could calm him. He squatted on the ground, holding his head between his knees, pretending not to hear. In spite of this, Twalen continued talking.

"Do you remember, my son, when I used to call you by the nickname 'caterpillar'? You were a baby then, a little crawling thing. There's a woman down there who's breastfeeding a caterpillar. . . ."

Mredah lifted his head and peered down to where his father was pointing.

"What has she done?" he asked impatiently, for he had the impression that whatever her story was, it had something to do with him.

"Fate plays strange tricks on us, and you can't avoid the consequences," said Twalen mysteriously.

"What has she done?" Mredah asked again, even more impatiently.

"She had only one child, and he died. Even though it wasn't her fault—it was just fate—nevertheless, she's being punished for having been a 'childless' woman. She's destined to breastfeed a caterpillar. Whenever she tries to get rid of it, the animal suckles away at her breast even more greedily. It's real torture. . . ."

"And what's that got to do with me?" Mredah inquired, more puzzled than ever.

"Well, it's up to you to figure that out," said Twalen, relieved to see that his son was more or less back to normal.

At that point, a demon pulled out his sword and savagely slashed at a man holding a hammer in his hand. The man fell to the ground, senseless.

"A silversmith who sold base metals in place of pure silver or gold! No use cheating others," Twalen remarked, shaking his head disapprovingly.

"There's another cowheaded cauldron!" Mredah suddenly shouted at the top of his voice. Twalen, staring at his son, wondered what had happened to make him raise his voice so.

"Nothing," said Mredah, as if he had read his father's thoughts. "Nothing," he repeated, trying to convince himself he was not a bit afraid.

Meanwhile the demons busily carried out their chores around the cauldron. One demon carried bundles of faggots back and forth, while Bhuta Ode Ode, as usual, continued blowing into the fire with all his might to keep it burning forever into eternity.

Not far away, the demon Bhuta Wide, who was in charge of dividing the souls into categories, was interviewing two souls who looked exactly alike.

"A pair of twins," noted Mredah eagerly, happy to have recognized the two men. "They always did their job as palm-wine tappers conscientiously, without ever being tempted to drink too much *tuak*."

Near the twins, an elderly woman with a pot on her head wandered about aimlessly. A demon kept close watch and followed her constantly.

"She was too greedy and selfish during her life," said Twalen matter-of-factly. "Now she can't have a single minute of rest. Day and night, she has to carry a pot about on her head."

"Is it heavy?" asked Mredah, slightly amused.

"Very heavy—heavy with all her past greed," Twalen replied.

"And there's another woman in solitary confinement," Mredah sighed. "How sad. . . ."

"She had a dreadful character, you know, always scheming behind her husband's back. Now she's alone, just as she deserves to be," Twalen declared.

At the sight of Jogormanik, father and son fell into silence. So awe-inspiring was his appearance that no one, after seeing him once, could ever mistake him for anyone else. Just then, he was harshly reprimanding a man who had been notorious for his untrustworthiness. He told lies his entire life, not for any particular reason, but just because it was a habit he enjoyed.

Behind Jogormanik stood an ugly little creature, a man who had been turned into a dwarf. The only feature that had retained its normal size was his head.

"What a huge head!" Twalen marveled.

"What a small body!" murmured Mredah.

"That's what conceited and arrogant people get. They think they're the best, that they don't need anything or anybody. You mustn't refuse what people have to offer—help, gifts or even good advice." Twalen drew a deep breath. As he spoke, he unconsciously touched his body here and there, as if to reassure himself that its size was unchanged.

"What a beautiful couple!" Mredah exclaimed out of the blue. (Obviously he wanted to change the subject in order to turn his father's attention away from the dwarf and his large head filled with conceit.)

"It's all appearances," remarked Twalen, glancing at the couple Mredah was pointing to.

"Why? What?"

"They are the sort of people called *mata kranjang.*"

"You mean to say that they have basket eyes?"

"Yes, eyes that look around in all directions—except where they should." Twalen clicked his tongue in disapproval. "You see, these two aren't husband and wife. They are lovers. She's probably the most disloyal wife you'll ever meet in your life. And the man, of course, didn't think twice about having an affair with another man's wife."

"It's all so complicated," Mredah puzzled. "A demon is about to leap on them with his sword. . . ."

"Not only on them, but also on that little sly-looking fellow who's trying to run away from the whole thing. Can you see him?"

"Of course, how could I miss him?" Mredah replied indignantly. "But who the devil is he?"

"He's the malignant spirit who orchestrated the whole mess, a matchmaker of illicit love affairs," Twalen explained. The words struck Mredah as rather obscure.

During the entire conversation between the royal clowns, Prince Bhima had remained silent. He was watching the events from a distance, absorbed in his own thoughts, withdrawn in deep meditation.

After a few minutes, the silence was once again shattered by Twalen's agitated voice.

"That's horrible! You wouldn't want to fall off that pole and be burned to a frazzle!"

"They'll land in the flames very soon. Look, a demon is about to jump on the pole. In they'll go," said Mredah.

"Do you see those babies watching? They tell the demon when to jump," Bhima said suddenly, addressing his servants as if he were emerging from a reverie.

But Twalen and Mredah had not noticed anything except the flames and the people about to fall into the fire.

"That explains it," Bhima continued. "The two women on the pole had abortions, and the man is the healer who performed the abortions. The two babies in the distance are the souls of those who were aborted. Life is sacred; not only is it everyone's duty to have children, but children themselves are sacred. At whatever cost, life has to go on. Destiny alone must decide our fate."

Bhima always spoke in solemn, awesome tones. After speaking he would immediately withdraw into silence as if nothing had happened. This is what he did now, leaving Twalen and Mredah free to go on chattering away.

"There's your friend Jogormanik again, son."

"He's not *my* friend! Are you crazy, Dad? Are you out of your mind? Have you lost your wits? Are you . . ."

"Shut up! Don't talk to me like that! I'm your father! How dare you speak to me like that! Remember the saw? Back and forth, back and forth. . . ."

"But he's not my friend, and *never* will be. Brrrr . . . what fangs!"

"You've got nothing to fear, son. There, once again he's praising the soul of a good woman. We often see him talking with good people." Twalen said this more as a question than a statement, for he wondered why Jogormanik's behavior here did not seem to correspond at all with the notorious picture everyone on earth painted of him.

"And just look at that other woman, poor thing," Mredah groaned. "The demon has been beating her with a club for the past hour."

"Well, that's what she deserves. Don't feel sorry for her, not a bit. She practiced black magic. There's an honest-to-goodness witch for you," Twalen pronounced.

"Brrrr . . . how scary! Help! Help!" Mredah cried. (At the mere utterance of the word "witch," he always tingled as if an electric shock or a bolt of lightning had actually struck his body.)

Just behind the witch, another demon was tormenting a man by pulling his hair with one hand and, with the other, brandishing a sword above his head.

"That's how they punish a liar, by taunting him and keeping him in constant fear that his head might be chopped off with a single blow," said Twalen.

At that moment, as if providing a backdrop for the scenes of the witch and the liar, two peculiar characters emerged: a man and a dwarf. They were running away, apparently hoping to escape the wrath of the demons.

"Wishful thinking!" Twalen and Mredah sang out together as if their thoughts were synchronized.

"They're wasting precious energy." Twalen shook his head knowingly. "It's too late. . . ."

"It's always too late," Mredah interrupted, glancing at his father, who stared back at him, astonished at his son's sudden flash of insight.

"If he had married—as every adult human ought to do—he wouldn't have to run like that now. Instead, by not establishing a family, he has remained, in a sense, a child," Twalen explained. "The dwarf is, in fact, his true self. If you refuse to assume responsibilities in life, how can you grow up and be looked upon as an adult?"

"Do you really mean that big man is still a child just like me?" Mredah was startled.

"Right. One part of his nature has never fulfilled itself. The very presence of that dwarf is his terrible punishment. By never being allowed to escape from that haunting shadow of himself, he's constantly reminded of his incompleteness. The demons won't let him forget, and that's sheer torture for him."

Twalen and Mredah were so engrossed in their discussion that they almost missed an extraordinary sight: a demon was crossing the landscape of Hell in a flamboyant cart with wheels as gigantic as the demon himself.

"Look! Look! Just look at those two men pulling the cart and being whipped at the same time. God help me not to do what led them to this!" shrieked Mredah, who was a lazy little fellow. Mredah's voice had now become so shrill that Prince Bhima could no longer ignore what his servants were saying.

"I bet that's the punishment inflicted on those who have tortured their buffaloes and other animals for the fun of it," Twalen guessed.

"Like catching a dragonfly and ripping off its wings, to watch its reaction," Mredah broke in.

"That is correct," said Bhima, in his usual cool, princely tone.

Every time Bhima spoke, which was rarely, Twalen and Mredah would remain speechless for a few moments afterward, as if there were absolutely nothing to add, as if the subject were completely exhausted. Their dialogue could only continue by shifting to a new topic with a new question.

"Sir, what about that man with a crown on his head? What does he have to smile about? Can't he see that the demon is about to slash him to pieces?" Twalen asked his master.

"That is not a smile. It is a grimace," corrected the prince. "He is suffering. The crown is too heavy for him. He was given the wrong cremation."

"Oh yes, I get it now." (Twalen was eager to show he had understood.) "He had a more elaborate send-off than his caste entitled him to. . . ."

"He should have made sure that his family would follow the custom," Mredah interrupted quickly, feeling he was being left out of the conversation.

"Precisely," said Bhima. "A peasant should not have a prince's tower built for himself, not even if he can afford it. This is the punishment dealt to all those who are social climbers. One should not trespass the boundaries imposed by one's birthright and, by so doing, play another man's role."

A few yards away Suratma, Yamaloka's record-keeper, was occupied with two men whose sin only Bhima could explain.

"It is forbidden for a brother and sister to take as husband and wife a man and woman who in turn are also brother and sister. This is called a crisscross marriage. To do this is as terrible as committing incest."

"Why?" asked Mredah, who saw no problem except that it was complicated to explain.

"It is all related to the issue of patriarchy. If one of the couples does not get along, then insoluble problems could arise between the families. And it is highly probable that one member of each couple will die prematurely," Bhima continued.

"It is all related to the issue of patriarchy," Twalen repeated pompously, as if he understood exactly what "the issue of patriarchy" meant.

As for Mredah, he was too absorbed in watching Suratma's doings to pay attention to Bhima's explanation. The demon was forcing each sinner to hold a *kris* by the blade with both hands. Then he would snatch the *kris* away, and the sinner's palms would bleed. As soon as the wounds healed, he would repeat the torture, again and again.

At this point, Mredah began to giggle uncontrollably. For a moment Twalen did not know what had happened, except that Prince Bhima had once again withdrawn from his retainers and was standing aloof in his usual silence.

"Look, Dad, look at that little fellow with the weird expression!" Twalen looked and almost instantly he too began to giggle uncontrollably.

"Yes . . . I know," he acknowledged, trying to conceal his amusement and appear more dignified.

The "little fellow with the weird expression" had always behaved very carelessly, having shown no respect for the members of his family or his friends. His habits were as weird as the look on his face. Whenever he was in the company of others, which was very often, he would fart and then giggle as if this were too funny for words. His friends, and especially his family elders, would complain and call him all sorts of names, but he never cared in the least. Even now, before the terrifying Jogormanik himself, he exhibited no fear whatsoever—at least, this was the impression he gave Twalen and Mredah, since he never ceased giggling; for all they knew, he was farting in Jogormanik's presence even now. He was indeed an amusing character, providing comic relief in the dreadful scene that was about to unfold before them.

Shifting their eyes, the clowns were appalled by their sudden awareness of the Kawah Blegede, a vast, silent lake of lava. Plunged up to their necks in the lake were the souls of countless people who had lost their minds and had committed all sorts of unspeakable sins. The fetid air spread over them like a suffocating blanket, oppressing them with the unbearable heat that steamed up from the lava. A faint humming mingled with the clouds of steam: the moaning of the souls. This sound reverberated as if it were coming straight from the bowels of the earth. Had it not been for their unending groans, one would have thought that all these souls were dead, for they showed no other sign of life.

Although, by this time, the strain of watching so much suffering had completely exhausted Twalen and Mredah, a new and unexpected sight whetted their curiosity and revived them: they now observed that, not far from the dreadful lake, all sorts of pleasant encounters were taking place. Accustomed to expecting only the worst till now, they were astounded when they saw Suratma and Jogormanik conversing exclusively with good souls.

Suratma was praising a man who had worked hard and honestly. A contractor by trade, the man had always built solid houses and given excellent advice to the *banjar,* or village council, on construction matters. Next to him, Jogormanik was congratulating a couple who had always respected each other. The man had been a devoted husband, and rightly so, because his wife had always been gentle and sweet to him and performed her household duties conscientiously and cheerfully without ever complaining.

91

But no sooner had the father and son relaxed a little—enjoying the restful presence of people who had always been good and who were on their way to Heaven—when something truly unpleasant caught their eyes. Twalen and Mredah both felt shivers run up and down their spines.

"He . . . he . . . hemorrhoids . . . ," Twalen stuttered. Mredah stammered, "Poo . . . poo . . . poor sss . . . sss . . . ssoul. . . ."

"The demon is pulling and squeezing them," Twalen gasped in terror.

"What . . . what has he done?" Mredah managed to blurt out.

"He was too careless, my son, too impolite, too disrespectful of gods and humans. He spread pollution."

"How? But how?"

"More than once he shat where he shouldn't have. . . ."

"On temple grounds?"

"So it seems. It's unforgivable, unforgivable," Twalen clucked disapprovingly, and just as a wet dog shakes itself to dry off, he shook his body as though trying to rid himself of the awful sensation he felt at the sight of this punishment for an unforgivable sin.

Meanwhile, yet another demon had just raised his spiked club against a farmer who had neglected to make the proper offerings to Dewi Sri, the goddess and guardian of rice fields. He had also cheated his neighbors by changing both the course of the irrigation canals and the boundaries of his land to his own advantage.

But the worst punishment of all was the one inflicted on the man who had never once performed his just share of work in the preparations for the village temple festival. His sole occupation in life had been to continually gorge himself. Cleverly, he would hide somewhere and spend all his time stuffing himself with the delicious food prepared specially for village festivals and intended for offerings to the gods or for sharing at the community banquets.

Twalen and Mredah, themselves incorrigible gluttons, were horrified, for they immediately identified with this sinner. As usual, they began to quake with fear.

"Look, Dad," squeaked Mredah with agitation, "they are pounding him. . . ."

"They'll make *sate* out of him." Twalen had a bad case of jitters.

"And the demons will chew him up and swallow him," added Mredah, who suddenly, for the first time in his life, had lost all taste for that indescribable delicacy called *sate*.

These depressing thoughts about food—for thoughts about food restrictions are always depressing—were brightened by the appearance of a lovely woman.

"That's Istri Lui," observed Twalen at once. ". . . the most beautiful and *best* wife of all," he added, emphasizing the word "best." Istri Lui was accompanied by her female servant, who sat on the same low level as Delem and Sangut, the retainers of Hell and bitter enemies of Twalen and Mredah. Jogormanik was also present, standing off to one side in a reverential attitude.

When Prince Bhima joined his retainers once again, Twalen and Mredah were still absorbed in Istri Lui's glowing beauty. But their blissful reverie ended abruptly with the sudden appearance of one of the angriest demons they had seen thus far. His roars resounded everywhere. Brandishing his sword, this monster was about to slay a man who had fallen at his feet.

"What has *he* done?" asked Twalen, who couldn't figure out what terrible sins the poor man must have committed. Again, only Bhima was able to shed light on the situation.

"That man slaughtered animals without caring about the prescribed ritual," Bhima explained in his severe tone. "One should never forget that animals are human beings who have taken on other shapes and forms. After one has looked after an animal with care, then the creature should rightly give up its life for its master. But during the slaughtering, one should always repeat this *mantra:* 'I am slaying you in order to free your soul. Do not take revenge on me.'"

No sooner had Bhima finished his explanation than another mystifying scene took place before Twalen and Mredah's eyes. Just as before, Suratma was torturing a man by forcing him to hold a *kris* by the blade and then pulling it suddenly away. The hapless sinner's palms were open wounds.

"It is a grave sin to carry a *kris* without its appropriate case, just for the purpose of frightening people," Bhima said gravely. "Only bandits do that. Only bandits misuse the blade of a *kris.*"

By now, Twalen and Mredah's heads truly buzzed with confusion. Many of the sins for which people were being punished were new to them. For the first time, they were learning about life from within. It was as if they were gazing into the very heart of life itself but could not grasp everything they saw there. All this was puzzling and painful and made them feel baffled about their own lives— past, present and future. *Everything* seemed to be forbidden!

To ease the tension a bit, Mredah asked, "Who's that old man squatting on the ground?"

This time Twalen knew everything about the old man, for his story was one of the many well-known folktales that the living never tired of telling and retelling. It had been handed down from father to son.

"Come on, son. . . . You know who he is," Twalen replied. "He's Gunung Lamed, the rich man . . ."

". . . who, one day, while working in one of his countless rice fields," Mredah readily recited, "noticed that one of his countless buffaloes was hungry. So he went off to look for some food. But on his way, a terrible misfortune occurred, and he fell to the ground, dead. When he reached Swarga, he brought with him all his fortune, in a box filled with gold. The demons, of course, took the box away and left him there waiting for god-knows-what. When they finally returned, they offered him two boxes: one was heavy and intricately carved, while the other was light and made of ordinary wood. To test his honesty and make sure he had not acquired his wealth in devious ways, Jogormanik and Suratma, who were in charge of this particular matter, ordered him to choose one of the boxes. The old man chose the light box of ordinary wood, thereby proving his honesty and humility."

"They are still questioning him." Twalen felt indignant. "They ought to let him go. . . . They could at least be polite with him after all they've put him through."

Twalen's last words faded into oblivion as, out of the blue, Mredah blurted out one of his typical exclamations, which once again took his father by surprise.

"*Look!* Dad! Oh, my god! *Look!*" he shrieked, torn between an intense desire to cover his eyes and a strangely irrepressible urge to gaze at what he so dreaded seeing. Neither Twalen nor Mredah—nor even Prince Bhima—could keep their eyes off the two men whose genitals were being burned by demons with flaming torches.

"My dear friends," warned Bhima, "you can see for yourselves that here is an extremely grave sin, to be avoided at all cost. This is the fate awaiting everyone who worships physical pleasure above everything else. These men tried to seduce not only their friends' wives but—just imagine!—even their own sisters."

"Got the message . . . ," Twalen muttered. Meanwhile Mredah, still a bit young for such things, wondered what "physical pleasure" really meant. (For him, physical pleasure was all concentrated in the taste of *sate* and sweet cakes, and thus he could not figure out why the demons were not burning the two men's mouths. He finally concluded there must be some major misunderstanding that had escaped everyone's notice.)

Both father and son, though for entirely different reasons, were profoundly shaken by the punishment inflicted on those two men who had "played around" too much. Twalen could not stand still and was jumping about in a most undignified manner, as if the entire lower part of his body were on fire. Mredah could not keep from holding his mouth wide open and sucking in air, as if he had eaten something unbearably hot and spicy.

"*Fire! Fire!*" the two were shouting at the top of their voices. Mredah was the first to calm down.

"Fir-r-r-re!" he trailed off in a much softer voice, for now he was no longer referring to the burning sensation he had felt in his mouth, but to a scene below in Hell that drew his attention precisely because it involved fire. Twalen, who by then had also calmed down, followed the direction of Mredah's gaze and indeed saw fire: a halo of flames encircling the head of a man whom a demon was tormenting with a torch.

"An arsonist getting his share of fire," Twalen perceived. "I bet he's regretting every bit of his evil and sick behavior! Instead of trying to resolve disputes wisely and diplomatically, that man always took his anger out on people by setting their houses on fire. . . ."

"And now he has to bear the torture of being constantly set on fire himself," added Mredah, unusually serious.

Nearby another drama was unfolding. A man holding a sharp spur in his right hand was desperately trying to escape the clutches of a demon who had already struck him with a sword. Twalen and Mredah immediately recognized this person as a cockfighting addict, notorious for his dishonesty. He had often attached the spur of his cock's leg so crookedly that the cock was sure to lose; then, by betting on his opponent's cock, he would deviously win all the money.

"Dishonesty, like corruption, is a real disease . . . ," murmured Twalen. Meanwhile, little Mredah was still so absorbed in the sight of the flames around the arsonist's head that he seemed deaf and dumb. But this last remark of his father's roused him.

"Fire! Fire!" he shouted again, though less forcefully than before.

"Yes, fire!" echoed Twalen, pointing at the soul of yet another sinner in the distance.

"Again?" Mredah exclaimed, looking at his father inquisitively.

"Yes," Twalen replied. "Again. That man is no good. He chased women left and right. . . ."

"Left and right," Mredah mumbled to himself, his eyes fixed on the flaming torch with which a demon was caressing the penis of the poor soul in question.

"He made too many marriage proposals, a real rake, never physically satisfied, always hungry for more," Twalen went on.

"For more of what?"

"For women, women and more women," intoned Twalen, as though chanting a litany. But Mredah had already been distracted by the fate of someone else nearby, whose situation seemed quite the opposite. An enraged sow was savagely attacking a man who had never married. Putting work before everything else in life, he had never had time for women and therefore avoided marriage and all that comes with it: a wife, children and grandchildren.

"He neglected human and spiritual values and preferred material gain instead," Twalen grunted with disgust.

"He's wasting his time now," little Mredah commented, "trying to tempt the sow away from his legs by holding out those nutmeg sprigs. Nothing will persuade that sow to prefer a bit of nutmeg to his beefy legs."

"There's another lonely woman," Twalen remarked.

"Not again . . . ," sighed Mredah.

By now father and son had learned how to recognize certain types of people merely from their facial expressions. Disloyal, selfish or bad-tempered wives all resembled one another and were easily identified by the strange, bitter mood of isolation expressed in their eyes. Even the demons avoided them; loneliness and silence were their punishment.

A few yards away from the solitary disloyal wife, Twalen and Mredah witnessed a truly bizarre scene. Two fierce-looking demons, grasping a man by his arms and feet, were thrusting his body through an arch formed by a curved blade that was slowly closing in on him. Amazed at the sight of such an intricate torture mechanism, both father and son remained speechless. They had not fully realized how advanced Yamaloka was in its fiendish technology.

"It is called Somba Wesi, the Iron Gate," Prince Bhima explained readily, seeing the perplexed expressions on his servants' faces. "This is the punishment for thieves. It symbolizes the opening in the wall of the house through which the thief sneaked when he committed his grave sin."

But what followed was beyond everybody's imagination. Suratma was closely supervising a demon engaged in punishing a woman whose breasts were indescribably beautiful. The demon was inserting a flaming torch into her vagina.

"She was too hot to have it, and now she has it hot!" Twalen was pleased at his own wit. Mredah, perplexed, stared at his father.

"Too hot to have what?"

"Men, men and more men," Twalen replied matter-of-factly.

"A whore?" Mredah asked. It was Twalen's turn to be startled; he wondered where on earth his son had learned such a word.

"Sort of . . . ," he murmured vaguely.

"And what about that other woman over there? What has *she* done?" little Mredah tirelessly questioned. "Why is the demon slicing her tongue to ribbons?"

"She wanted power. She practiced black magic, my son."

"A *witch*! Help me, god! I hate them! I hate them!" Mredah began to quiver like a leaf in the wind.

"Calm down, calm down, my son. You've got nothing to fear. You are here, she's there. You're alive, she's dead. All you have to remember for your own good is that it's evil to manipulate people and play with their lives."

As soon as Mredah realized that his father was speaking the truth and that he himself was alive while the witch was a harmless soul suffering the consequences of her misdeeds, he became less agitated. He remained remarkably calm even when he observed the gruesome scene that immediately followed: some demons were tormenting a man who had committed murder.

"There's not much to say when murder is the issue." Twalen, too, was surprisingly calm. "That man has killed, and no one on earth has the right to take away another's life."

The punishment inflicted on the murderer was dreadful. Two demons, one on each side, were plunging their *kris* so deeply into his chest that blood gushed in torrents from the wounds. Because he had committed murder, he had to undergo, in return, the horror of being murdered over and over again.

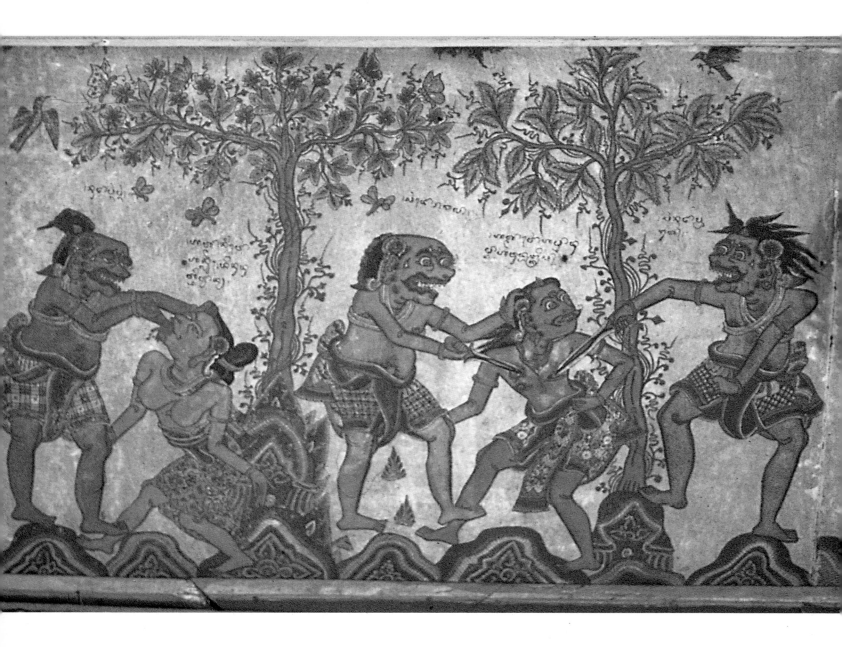

For a long time, Twalen and Mredah had not seen Jogormanik, and they were just on the verge of forgetting all about him when that awesome demon reappeared. As they had often observed him do before, he was bidding farewell to a soul who had fulfilled his period of punishment and was now setting off on the journey to Heaven. Jogormanik was showing him the way, so that he would not get lost god-knows-where.

No words could adequately describe what thoughts passed through the two clowns' minds as they squatted on the side of the mountain and witnessed the innumerable awful scenes of Hell below. Their discussions were often interspersed with long silences. Meanwhile, Prince Bhima sat there, proud and unshaken, without a trace of fear. Twalen was the first to break the silence this time.

"Get it while you can, son," he whispered to Mredah. "If you want to be well supplied later on, you'd better stock up on good things now. That's what I think."

Mredah was not listening, but rather was completely absorbed in mumbling unintelligibly to himself. Since he often muttered in this way, it was not in itself particularly surprising. This time, however, Twalen became alarmed that his son had lost his mind.

"Tri kaya pari sudha," muttered Mredah, "better known as Tri kaya paari suddha . . . or as they say, Tri kaya pari suddha. . . . Those who know wouldn't be caught without their TKPS. It's their rock, their foundation, and that goes for people like us, Dad. . . ."

Twalen was utterly baffled, for he could not understand a word Mredah was saying. Once again, he asked himself the recurring question of his life: "Is my son a genius, or is he an unfortunate fool?"

"What does Tri kaya pari sudha, or paari suddha, or pari sudda, stand for?" he asked, trying to sound natural.

"What do you think?" responded Mredah.

Twalen, just about on the verge of a nervous breakdown, shouted, "That's what I want to know from you! *Tell me!*"

"It's the big three, Dad. Do, think, speak. The three are really one. You should know that," Mredah replied immediately.

The answer was simple, but Twalen could not figure out what the big three had to do with the tortures of Hell.

"Before you do anything," Mredah went on, "think about it. Once you've thought about it, talk about it, get it all lined up. Once you've thought about it and talked about it, do it. If you try to do something without thinking it through and talking it out, it's sure to fall apart. Then you'll have to bear the consequences. But if all you do is talk, then the doing never gets done. Tri kaya pari suddha, even though some people pronounce it in other ways. It all adds up. It's the only way to finish what you've started, and then have a harmonious life."

Even after such a long monologue, Twalen was not quite sure how all this related to Hell, but he was more and more convinced that Mredah was blessed with a touch of genius. He was all too aware of his son's shortcomings: Mredah, admittedly, was an impudent scoundrel, quite a cowardly one at that, always complaining and accusing others when anything went wrong. Nevertheless, Twalen felt, proudly, that although Mredah's words seemed like the chaotic ramblings of a lunatic erupting out of the blue, these words expressed some profound truth.

"There's no way to measure all the harm that's done. It all comes out in the end," Twalen remarked, changing the subject altogether. "Whatever goes up is bound to come down sooner or later. Like a wheel turning. Too much of anything will kill you."

Suddenly Twalen and Mredah's philosophical ramblings were interrupted by the most frightening words they had ever heard.

"Let us go!" Bhima ordered.

By then, the prince was already descending the steep path that wound its way down into Hell.

Only a few minutes had elapsed—or at least so it seemed to Twalen and Mredah—when they found themselves face to face with none other than Jogormanik himself, in flesh and blood. At his side stood Delem and Sangut, their sworn enemies.

"Unfortunate soul, you stranger, you are not a true soul. You are still raw, still a human. What is your name? Where do you come from? And what are you doing here?" Jogormanik bellowed at Bhima.

"I am the second child of the renowned warrior family, the Pandawas. Bhima is my name. I have come to search for the souls of my father, King Pandu, and my second mother, Dewi Madri. I will rescue them from the boiling waters of the cauldrons of Hell. Wherever they are, I will save them and bring them peace," declared the prince, resolute and solemn.

"Bhima, you cannot speak like that and get away with it," retorted Jogormanik, struggling to control his temper. "The workings of this place must not be disturbed. Go back home to your own kingdom, or you will die. The living do not belong here, and the fate of the dead cannot be changed. Your parents are no exceptions. Go away!"

But Bhima refused to go away; quite the contrary. Several souls who were waiting for judgment nearby had overheard his words, and they gathered in front of the Pandawa prince to pay homage to him, as if their fate were now in his hands.

But before he even had time to think of some way to persuade Jogormanik to let him in, a phalanx of armed demons lined up before him like an impenetrable wall. Raising their weapons high, the demons showed their teeth and howled with anger, like rabid dogs.

Then they attacked. Countering them, Bhima swung his famous club left and right, right and left. So many arrows flew that the sky grew as dark as midnight. But the arrows that hit Bhima's chest bounced off him like miraculous boomerangs, killing the very demons who had fired them. Even Jogormanik could not save himself from Bhima's wrath, and he fell to the ground.

Twalen and Mredah were caught in the midst of the battle. Suddenly—god knows how!—they, too, had become valiant warriors, fighting with all their might. While Twalen pierced the hearts of many demons with his immensely long spear, Mredah wielded his knife as if it were a gigantic magic sword.

Soon, Bhuta Abang and his assistants fled in terror, leaving the cauldrons of Hell unguarded.

At one point Twalen found himself face to face with Delem, his age-old enemy. After savage combat, he impaled Delem with his spear. One after the other, the demons who had not had time to run away fell wounded or dead upon the ground. In the midst of it all, Bhima remained the dominant figure, and his invincible valor so overwhelmed the army of demons that at last the few who remained fled in terror. The way into Hell lay wide open.

Bhima knew he could not afford to waste a single moment; he must fulfill his mission quickly, before Yama, the mighty god and master of Hell, had been informed of his invasion. Thus, Bhima entered Hell in great haste, with Twalen and Mredah running to keep up with him. Immediately he proceeded to tear Yamaloka asunder, wreaking unimaginable havoc. He even overturned the enormous cauldron of Tambra Goh Muka so that its boiling contents poured out, not only releasing dozens of souls but, at the same time, extinguishing the fire.

Free at last from the horrid boiling waters, the souls worshiped Bhima as if he were a god. Twalen and Mredah felt like little gods themselves as they sat proudly next to their master.

Seated in lotus position, the prince strained his eyes, searching for King Pandu and Dewi Madri among the grateful souls; but he could not find them. All the souls looked identical, with the males being indistinguishable from the females. He decided that the only possible solution would be to free all the souls in Hell so that Pandu and Madri would necessarily be released.

While all these thoughts were taking shape in Bhima's mind, in his palace Lord Yama was receiving the news of the Pandawa invasion. The demon Nirganetra, who looked very much like Togtogsil, together with Delem and Sangut and a group of demon generals, was agitatedly describing what had occurred.

"Bhima has not heeded Jogormanik's warning. He is destroying Hell and now is heading toward your palace, my Lord. Not only is he running amok, destroying everything, causing trouble left and right, but he is even turning the souls loose. My Lord, Hell will never be the same again. This man is a menace. Just imagine, he has the audacity to overturn the cauldrons and throw everyone out. What nerve! In Hell's name, stop him before it is too late. *Kill him! Kill him!*"

The news so enraged Yama that his body swelled up like a balloon, and his face turned so red that it looked as if it had been scorched by a flaming torch.

"Call him!" he ordered. "I wish to speak to him in person. At once! *Now!*" His voice thundered through every corner of Hell.

A little later, Bhima strode into Yama's presence. Only Twalen accompanied him, since Mredah had not been admitted to the palace and was obliged to wait outside.

"Bhima of the Pandawas, I order you to leave my kingdom at once!" roared the god like an angry lion. "This is the order of Yama, king of Hell. This is *my* order!"

"Great god Yama, mighty Lord," Bhima replied unshaken, "I have come here to free my parents, King Pandu and Dewi Madri, and I will not leave until my mission is completed."

"This means war!" Yama announced. "Heed my words, Bhima. My servants will kill your servants, and as for you, I will slaughter you with my own hands."

By the time Bhima and Yama had finished with their confrontation, the army of Hell had already lined up, ready for combat. As commanding general, Yama himself, astride his huge spotted elephant, gave the final orders. The army stormed from the palace in frenzied pursuit of Bhima, who, accompanied by Twalen and Mredah, was rushing back toward the cauldrons.

Soon the sky of Hell flashed with thousands of arrows, as if the demons were staging a stupendous display of fireworks. Bhima turned to confront the advancing army. In the face of such danger as would have reduced even the bravest man to a quivering mass of jelly, the heroic Bhima grew bolder and mightier than ever. He blazed with the fierce power of the summer sun and leaped with such incredible agility that he evaded even the most determined attacks.

At one point he even managed to disappear altogether from the demons' sight. Only Twalen and Mredah knew where he was and what he was doing. While they fought, they were also watching his exploits from afar. The prince was bravely overturning yet another cauldron filled to the brim with souls.

Just as before, the freed souls lined up before him to pay homage to their savior. Soon the devoted Twalen and Mredah joined their master, eager to participate in this act of obeisance, which filled them with such reverential joy and renewed their courage and energy.

A moment later, the indefatigable Bhima sped as swiftly as a falcon toward another churning cauldron to overturn it. This time Twalen and Mredah helped as best they could, and they tingled with excitement when they saw the souls pouring out by the dozens, by the hundreds, by the thousands.

Once again, the souls sang in chorus to Bhima, "Thank you, dear Lord, for saving us. Thank you a thousand times over, five thousand times over. . . ."

Meanwhile, back at his field headquarters, Yama was following the progress of the battle and was growing increasingly horrified at the disastrous turn of events.

"This Bhima is incomprehensible. He does not seem to have a normal body of flesh and blood. Why, his very body acts like a shield, repelling arrows and bending swords!" the demons reported with amazement. "And even his idiotic servants possess extraordinary strength. With all this furious fighting, the army of Hell is beginning to show signs of exhaustion."

134

The battle was indeed furious. At one point it looked as if Twalen and Mredah might be overcome by the demons' savagery. Three of the most vicious demons Twalen had yet encountered suddenly leaped from ambush and, attacking en masse, pinned him to the ground. He felt their jagged fangs tearing into the flesh of his chest, and one of their swords missed his heart by only a few inches. As for poor Mredah, at that very moment a demon pounced on him from behind and began gnawing at his little body like a famished predator. Despite their apparently hopeless dilemma, the two Pandawa retainers were smiling ironically. The ferocious attacks soon dwindled to mere child's play, for all at once, as though infused with miraculous strength, the two clowns wriggled from their captors' clutches and slashed the demons to shreds.

For Bhima, the entire battle appeared to be no more than a game. Even when he was face to face with Jogormanik himself, the prince met his blows with such ease that the demon minister's sword seemed a mere toy weapon with a rubber blade. Bhima's strength surpassed the highest flights of the imagination. On and on he fought, without showing the slightest sign of fatigue. His muscles, in fact, grew stronger and stronger as his impatience and determination increased. With one powerful blow, his club would smash a whole squadron of attackers into tiny pieces; with another, it would knock over an entire regiment as if they were toy soldiers. At the same time, his foot would be kicking over another cauldron. Then, like a bird of prey, he would leap back into the heart of the battle and knock off a few more demon heads. The enemy arrows, on hitting his chest, simply tickled his skin. None of the demons could match his power; one by one, they sank to the ground, their brains spilling out under the blows of the club. In the midst of the fighting, Twalen and Mredah, filled with astounding courage and strength, behaved like true warriors. And, as they watched their master's exploits, they swelled with pride at being his retainers.

The demons' situation grew so alarming that finally the god Yama himself felt obliged to engage in battle. The time had come to kill Bhima and restore order in Hell. Enough of this nonsense! Why, rumors were beginning to spread that Bhima was determined to save the whole of mankind from Hell! As he fumed with rage, Yama's face turned black and steam poured from his ears. So great was his fury that it transformed the very sky of Hell into a reflection of him—a heavy, black cloud of heat that spread as far as the eye could see. The god left his headquarters wearing his favorite crown. It glittered for miles around, announcing his decision to fight.

Soon strange rumors reached every corner of Hell.

"The Lord has killed Bhima! The prince squealed like a stuck pig. . . . Bhima is dead!"

And the whispering went on: "There is no place to bury him. No graveyard, nothing. It's a real problem—a tough one for everybody. There's never been an actual dead body in Swarga before. No one knows how to handle a corpse."

But, fortunately, these rumors were a pack of lies; the truth turned out to be quite the opposite. Bhima was in perfect health—it was Yama who was squealing like a stuck pig. With his powerful hand, Bhima was gripping the god's throat so tightly that Yama was gasping, terrified he would be strangled. Never before in his life had Yama imagined that he could ever feel fear, let alone be in actual danger of dying. He, Yama, the god of the dead! And here he was, begging for mercy!

"Please do not kill me! Do not do it!" he was blubbering, desperately trying to escape. His servants, Delem and Sangut, could do nothing to help him.

"This is it, Lord Yama," Twalen smiled wryly. "The end. Your time is fast running out. You're about to become dust and ashes."

"Let me go! Please let me go!" Yama pleaded, his strength ebbing and his voice fading.

"I am here to save the souls of my parents, Pandu and Madri, nothing more," Bhima said. "Bring them to me, and I will let you go. This is your only chance."

"Yes . . . you will have Pandu and Madri. Yes . . . you will have your way. . . . I will give you the souls you want . . . ," Yama whispered feebly. By now he was choking with effort to get his breath, his veins bulging. Everything was growing dim before his eyes. At Yama's words, Bhima immediately let go of his throat.

The god hurried back to his palace. Seated on his buffalo throne, he managed, with considerable effort, to regain his majesty and dignity. Then, in thundering, regal tones, he announced the end of the war and his decision to let Bhima have his way.

But communications had broken down, and the royal edict did not reach every corner of Hell. Bhima suddenly found himself surrounded by a gang of armed demons who, leaping out of nowhere, attacked him with unbelievable violence. Caught by surprise, the prince fought them all the more fiercely and slaughtered the whole band. The moans of the dying demons echoed far and wide, like the rumble of erupting volcanoes.

In the confusion of the ambush, little Mredah lost sight of Twalen. Surrounded by a circle of demons that began to close in on him menacingly, he fought like a crazed scarecrow. All he could see was the demons' swords. The sky above him had become a battlefield of blades.

By now Bhima was convinced that Yama had cheated him and had not kept his promise to end the war and let him have Pandu and Madri. But just as Bhima was overturning another cauldron, the god Yama himself appeared.

"Here are your parents, Prince Bhima. Look deeply into the boiling lava of this cauldron, and you will see them!" Yama shouted, pointing at the lava flowing out of the cauldron.

Bhima stared unblinking at the lava. And indeed, there among many other souls were Pandu and Madri, floating out of the cauldron.

"I hereby give you the soul of your father, King Pandu, and the soul of your second mother, Dewi Madri, so that I may continue to live in peace," Yama said loudly. Then he instantly vanished, with only the brilliant glitter of his god's halo remaining visible.

Pandu and Madri were sleeping, their arms entwined. They had not aged; it was evident that their beauty and their love for each other had remained intact. Twalen bowed to them and said, "Greetings, my Lord . . . my Lady. . . ."

Mredah addressed them reverently. "Great Lord, may I introduce myself in case you have forgotten me. I am your loyal clown, the clown of your beloved descendants. I am here to honor you, my Lord and my Lady."

Prince Bhima said nothing. His face beamed with happiness as he gathered Pandu and Madri in his arms. Now that he had found them, he was anxious to hurry home, for he knew that a great task still awaited him if he was to complete his mission: Pandu and Madri were now safe, but they had no power of speech, and somehow Bhima would have to help them recover it.

Several souls joined the royal party for the journey back. Pandu and Madri were carried in a litter, as if they were in a stately procession.

But Twalen had noticed that something was wrong.

"They cannot respond, although they do seem to feel and perceive. What can we do? What can be done?" he wondered.

In fact, their breathing was the only sign of life in Pandu and Madri; otherwise they seemed dead. Not once during the entire journey did they open their eyes. The truth was that their souls were still far from pure. The couple were free only in appearance, not in actuality. Within, Pandu and Madri were still polluted by sin.

The group finally reached the Sarayu River, where the crocodiles again helped them to cross. Soon Bhima, Twalen and Mredah recognized the familiar landscape of the Pandawa kingdom. By sunset, they reached the palace.

As soon as the royal procession entered the throne room, Queen Kunti, accompanied by her eldest son Yudhisthira, her younger son Arjuna, and the twins Nakula and Sahadewa, rushed forward to welcome King Pandu and Dewi Madri, Bhima and the loyal Twalen and Mredah. When Bhima embraced his mother and brothers, their spirits, which had protected him on the journey, left him and reentered the bodies of each member of the family.

"We honor and respect you," the twins said to Madri, their mother. She heard, but could not convey the deep emotion she felt. Then the whole family bowed before Pandu and Madri.

"We have paid our respects, but it does not seem to help," Yudhisthira remarked with concern. "They are still not alive."

Kunti was moved with compassion and wept. When she was finally able to speak again, her white hair glistened like a crown of pearls struck by sunbeams.

"We must all continue to pay homage to them. Let us not worry about other things. We must pray." Her words carried the power and dignity of a royal command. They all prayed before the silent couple. Only Bhima remained aloof and did not bow. His brothers, observing this, went over to him.

"Bow down before your parents, Bhima. Do not wait till tomorrow; do it now. All of us must pay homage. Do not leave things undone!" admonished Yudhisthira, the eldest, speaking on behalf of his brothers.

"It is true, they are my parents. But do not expect me to bow to them, or for that matter to anyone else," Bhima replied. "That is something I have never done, neither at home nor in the holiest temple. I bow only to Sanghyang Acintya, the god of all gods, the ultimate force embracing all forces. As for all the other gods below him, not even the holiest among them will ever receive my complete homage, here or anywhere."

Meanwhile Twalen and Mredah chattered away. "No use insisting with Bhima. They should know him by now. If he doesn't want to do something, he won't do it. That's all," said Twalen in a worried tone.

"Our Lord always knows exactly what he wants, and that's that," said Mredah apprehensively.

The clowns' comments were suddenly interrupted by an occurrence that no one, not even they, could have imagined. As stubborn as Bhima was in his refusal to bow to Pandu and Madri, his brothers were equally stubborn in insisting that he *should* bow. Not only did they insist verbally, but when they found that words were insufficient, they even used physical force on him: from behind his back, raising his arms and holding his hands in a gesture of prayer, they attempted to change his mind.

Bhima's reaction was immediate and violent. He leaped back enraged and, brandishing his club, threatened to kill his brothers.

"Oh, god! Not this! Oh, Heaven! Oh, Hell!" squeaked Twalen and Mredah together, cowering in a corner and trying to make themselves smaller than they already were.

Queen Kunti, who knew her son's difficult character and hot temper, immediately intervened.

"Son, your brothers mean well. Throw your club away. They mean no harm," she pleaded in the warmest, most affectionate tone of voice the clowns had ever heard. Instantly Bhima calmed down. His brothers as well as Twalen and Mredah gave a deep sigh of relief.

But Pandu and Madri, clasping each other tightly, still showed no signs of improvement. Even Bhima's angry shouts had not roused them from their deep slumber; they had never even stirred. They were as if bewitched by some evil spell.

Now the queen, who understood a great deal about life, expressed her thoughts. She addressed herself to all, but to Bhima in particular.

"Pandu and Madri are not permitted to enter Heaven in their present condition. Unless they can drink the holy water of the gods, they will not be able to attain peace. Do not fight, my sons. More important things must be done."

Bhima immediately understood what his mother meant—in fact he had known it all along and was prepared for it.

"Bhima," the queen continued, this time looking straight at him, "go to Heaven and bring back the Tirta Amrta, the holy water of immortality. They are in tremendous need of it. You must go."

Twalen and Mredah glanced at each other.

"Our Lord," they whispered in unison, "if we don't hurry up, all our work in Hell will have been in vain. We must leave right now," they said, enjoying the idea of being on the road again. Journeys to Swarga were not that bad after all. The clowns had become adventurous at heart and now rather enjoyed the thrill of a risky life. They saw themselves not simply as citizens of the Pandawa kingdom, but as citizens of both worlds, Earth and Swarga. As a result, they had begun to feel at ease everywhere.

And so it was that Bhima, with Twalen and Mredah at his side, left the palace once again, this time headed to Heaven.

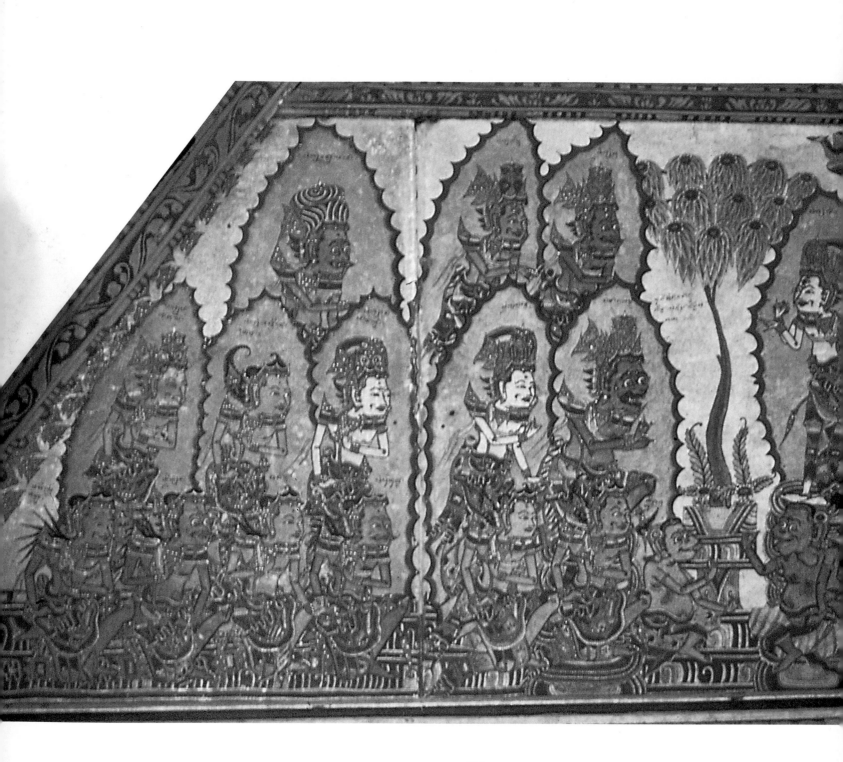

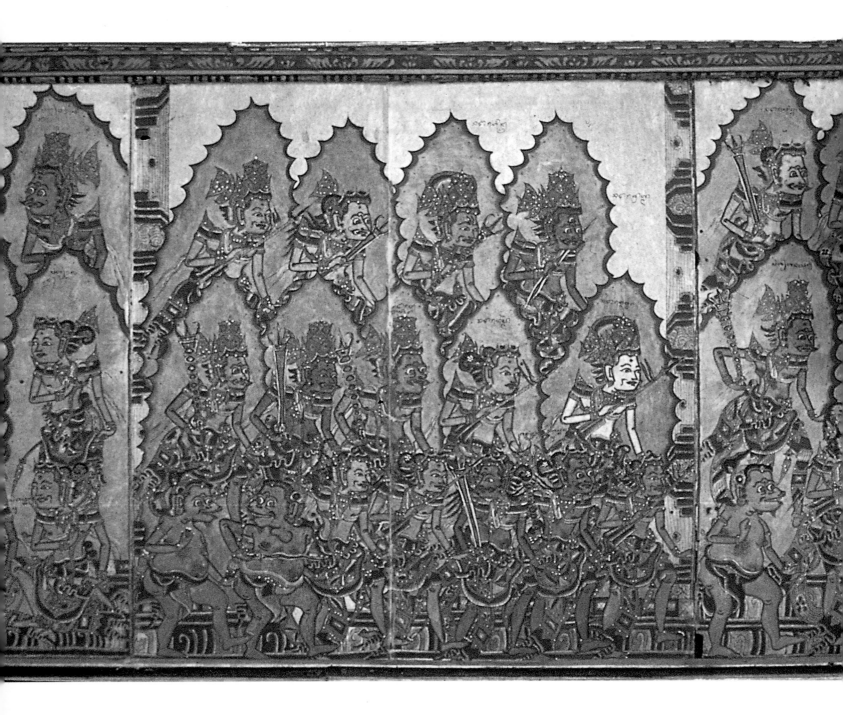

Bhima's arrival in Heaven caused such a great commotion that the most prominent gods met in conference. Presiding over the assembly stood Siwa, most powerful of the gods, he who holds the world together with his four arms and sees everything with his third eye. Gathered around him were the other nine chief gods: Iswara, Lord of the East; Maheswara, Lord of the Southeast; Brahma, Lord of the South; Rudra, Lord of the Southwest; Mahadewa, protector of the Earth and Lord of the West; Sangkara, Lord of the Northwest; Vishnu, Lord of the North; Sambhu, Lord of the Northeast; and finally Yama, Lord of Hell. Delem and Sangut, the retainer-clowns of Swarga, took their place beside Yama.

Siwa opened the meeting.

"Bhima, prince of the Pandawa kingdom, has invaded Heaven in order to obtain the Tirta Amrta. Our holy water is not meant to be drunk by humans, nor is it meant for the souls in Hell. But Bhima refuses to leave. We *must* stop him."

Although Siwa spoke with his customary calm and melodious voice, the deep furrows on his brow and the strange gleam in his eyes made it evident that he was extremely agitated and angry. After all, this was the first time that the peace of Heaven had been disturbed.

"I order all the gods to take battle formation at once and prepare to attack the invader!" Siwa commanded sternly. Immediately the gods lined up for battle, determined to dissuade the Pandawa prince from pursuing his sacrilegious mission.

A few minutes later, the gods launched their attack on the valiant Bhima and his clowns from two directions. Magic arrows flashed across the sky like lightning. Twalen and Mredah dashed about with their weapons like little supermen, making it impossible for the gods to catch or wound them. Bhima's strength was beyond description, beyond anything the gods had ever witnessed.

Suddenly god Gana, Siwa's elephant-headed son, arrived with reinforcements. But Bhima was truly invincible. He continued fighting, oblivious of the fact that—aside from his clowns—he was alone, waging war with hundreds of gods. As if he were confronting not an army of gods but only a single, feeble human being, Bhima battled without the slightest trace of fear. And, miraculously, the gods' weapons, even though they were imbued with the most powerful magic, failed to inflict any wound whatsoever—not even a scratch—on the hero. Truly, Bhima's body was like an iron wall. When arrows struck his chest, they merely bent or broke.

Even in Heaven, Bhima's power was unmatched.

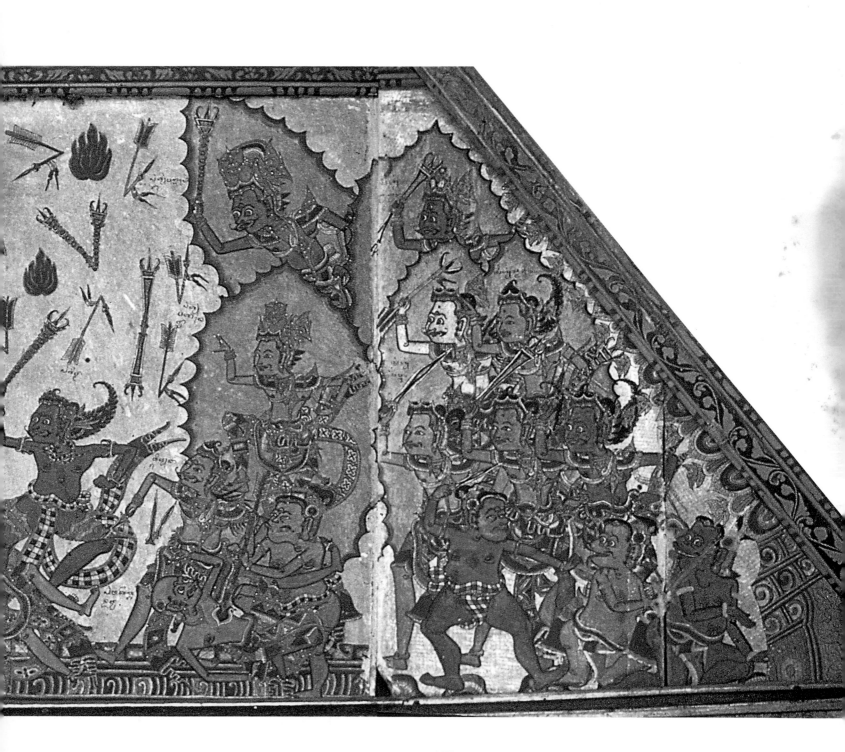

While all this was going on, Siwa, Iswara, Brahma, Mahadewa, Vishnu and several other gods decided to hold another emergency meeting. Never before had such a battle transpired in Heaven. The assembled gods felt such anxiety that the very air around them quivered with tension. Delem and Sangut, the servants of Swarga, went off to one side and conversed excitedly.

"Nothing frightens him, not even the power of the mighty gods," Delem said with astonishment.

"Bhima doesn't take no for an answer. He has lost his mind once again," whispered Sangut.

With all the gods standing pale-faced before him, Siwa declared, "There is no time to waste. I wish to speak to god Bayu. Summon him at once!"

God Bayu was none other than Bhima's real father, the god with whom Queen Kunti had used her special boon for the second time. Thus, it was just possible that Bayu might be able to persuade Bhima to leave Heaven in peace. Although till now Bhima would not listen to anyone else, even a god, perhaps he would heed his father. Siwa knew that Bayu held special power over his son because Bhima was part of him; therefore Bayu, if necessary, could neutralize that very part within himself.

As soon as Bayu heard that god Siwa wanted to see him, he rushed to the meeting hall. It was strange to see Bayu in front of Siwa, for Bayu and Bhima looked so much alike that one had the impression of seeing Bhima himself. The only feature that distinguished father from son was the golden divine halo surrounding Bayu's body.

Siwa and Bayu discussed at length the serious matter of Bhima's invasion and his quest for the holy water of immortality. Bayu was extremely distressed and ashamed of his son, and he promised Siwa he would do his utmost to stop Bhima and make him agree to return home.

Soon afterward, god Bayu met with his son Bhima, with no one else present except Twalen and Mredah. Squatting on the ground near their master, they were struck with awe on seeing the fabled god directly in front of them, close enough to touch.

"How's Lord Bayu going to handle all this? They really look like twins, don't they?" whispered little Mredah with amazement.

"Ssst . . . ," admonished Twalen, who did not want to miss a single word of Bayu's exchange with Bhima.

"My child," began Bayu, "no one but the gods and the souls of Heaven may drink the holy Tirta Amrta. The gods make no exceptions. You must return home. Bhima, this is no place for you."

"My Lord, my father, I will not go home before I have found the Tirta Amrta. I am sorry, but I cannot obey you. I am ready to fight again and again if necessary," Bhima replied, unmoved by his father's plea.

"I order you to go home. I command you to obey me. I am your father," said Bayu in a firm, angry voice.

The clowns kept absolutely silent, scarcely daring to breathe. They knew their master well and felt that something dreadful was about to happen, something that would surely lead their prince—as well as themselves—to disaster.

What Twalen and Mredah dreaded most was what actually did occur an instant later. Bayu had barely finished speaking when Bhima, with an astonishing display of hot-tempered impetuosity, suddenly raised his club against his father.

"Son, how dare you violate my word, the word of your heavenly father!" shouted Bayu, gripping Bhima's arm and halting it in midair. The clowns averted their eyes in fright and felt as if the whole of Heaven were about to fall upon them. And indeed, it almost did when Bayu, with just a single blow, a blow requiring no weapon, struck Bhima dead. The prince shuddered as if an electric current were flowing through his whole body. Then he bent down on his knees and fell silent. Twalen and Mredah, utterly shocked and dumbfounded, stood there frozen, their feet riveted to the ground, their heads spinning in pain and fear.

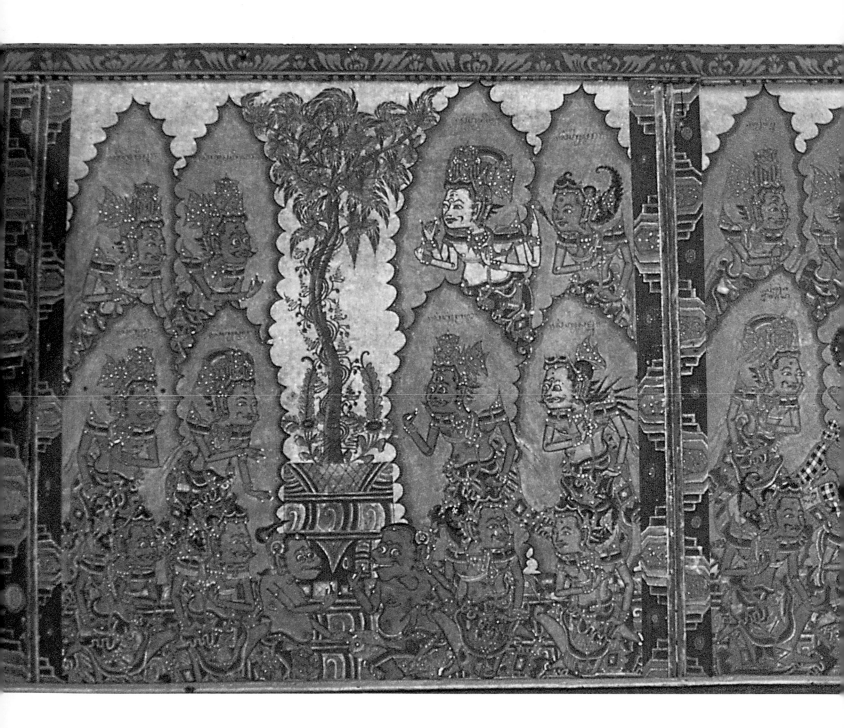

The very instant that Bhima was struck, darkness fell like a thick curtain, and all the souls of Heaven turned as pale as cadavers. They began to shuffle about listlessly, as if all their vitality and happiness had suddenly dissolved into nothingness. The animals, too, lost all their energy, and even the gods looked ill.

Many souls fell into troubled sleep, while others stood wavering under the trees as if drugged. Plants and trees drooped forlornly and faded. Heaven soon became as gray and empty and miserable as some days are on earth.

Bayu stood there speechless for a while, gazing at his beloved son. His pain was intense. He turned the matter over and over again in his mind and for a moment cursed Bhima's stubbornness, which had left him no choice but to destroy the part within himself that bore Bhima's name. His heart bled with sorrow as he stared at his son's body, motionless as a statue. Then he disappeared to weep bitterly in private.

Later that day, god Bayu gravely and sadly informed the other gods that Bhima was now helpless and no longer dangerous. He preferred not to mention the word "dead," for he loved his son dearly and could not reconcile himself to the disaster that had befallen Bhima.

Meanwhile Twalen and Mredah guarded their master's body, day after day, night after night, unaware that Heaven had been overcome with such lassitude. All they could think about was Bhima and about how they themselves could possibly live now without him. Too sad and frightened even to speak or to cry, they crouched in shocked silence, their eyes fixed on their master.

Then one night, something extraordinary happened. With the swiftness of a comet flashing across the starry sky, with the unexpectedness of a miracle, something occurred that took Twalen and Mredah completely by surprise. Just as they dozed off for a moment, they were suddenly awakened by a blinding light. To their amazement, they saw a brilliantly radiant white cloud hovering around Bhima, enveloping him like a blanket of luminous silk. And within the cloud's sinuous waves appeared Sanghyang Acintya, the god of all gods, the ultimate force embracing all forces.

"Bhima, come back to life. Let strength return to all that is weak," Acintya intoned, pronouncing each word slowly and distinctly.

Before the clowns could grasp what was taking place, Bhima rose and bowed, with every atom of his inner and outer self paying homage to the only god he truly revered.

"Thank you, my Lord," the prince said humbly. "Thank you."

By then Acintya had disappeared. As if nothing had happened, Bhima turned to his servants and said, "Come on, wake up, my friends. There is no time to waste. Let us go!"

"At your service, sir," the clowns chimed in unison, "at your service!"

And so it was that Bhima and his clowns stormed off once again through the gardens and palaces of Heaven in their search for the water of immortality.

Meanwhile all the gods and the souls of Heaven also had regained their strength. That very day the army of Heaven met Bhima and the Pandawa retainers in another hopeless battle. The prince was more courageous and mighty than ever, and his will was so invincible that nothing could prevent him from attaining his goal. The army of Heaven finally retreated in great confusion.

Heaven had fallen into utter chaos. Bewildered, the gods gathered around god Bayu. Bhima's name was on everybody's lips. No one knew what else to do. Rumors spread that this was the end of Heaven.

When the gods met again in solemn assembly, it was Bayu who spoke first: "Lord Siwa," he said, facing the powerful god, "I advise you to grant Bhima what he wants. Only you can give him the Tirta Amrta. No one in Heaven can match his strength. He is under the protection of the highest powers, and he has the determination of a giant."

God Siwa remained silent for a while and then concluded that he had no choice but to give Bhima what the prince most wanted.

"I will do as you wisely say, Lord Bayu," Siwa finally replied. "I will grant Bhima the Tirta Amrta." These words were followed by a moment of serenity, greater than any that Heaven had experienced in a long time.

A few hours later, when Bhima entered the heavenly conference hall presided over by Siwa, a sigh of relief spread through the air and was borne by the breeze across the great expanse of Heaven.

Standing beside his father Bayu, at a level below that of the most prominent gods to show his respect, Bhima could not take his eyes off the carved golden, winged goblet that Siwa held in his hands. Then the great god spoke. Twalen and Mredah stared and marveled at the beauty of the goblet and at the sound of Siwa's melodious voice.

"Bhima, take this goblet to your parents. It contains the holy water of immortality."

Bhima took the goblet and held it proudly in his hands.

"Thank you, Lord Siwa," the prince said, "thank you on behalf of my earthly father, King Pandu, and my second mother, Dewi Madri."

Twalen and Mredah could not conceal their emotion, and their eyes were shining with joy.

"Mission accomplished . . . ," little Mredah whispered to himself.

"Not yet," said Twalen, who had overheard his son's words. "Not yet. It will be accomplished only when we have returned to the palace and King Pandu and Dewi Madri have drunk the Tirta Amrta."

"They must be so thirsty by now . . . ," Mredah went on.

After bidding farewell to all the gods, and particularly to his heavenly father Bayu, Bhima prepared for the journey home.

"Let us leave at once," he said to his servants.

"At once!" echoed Twalen. "Come on, Mredah. Let's go!" he ordered his little son, who looked totally dazed and not at all ready to leave Heaven.

"Can't I stay? You go. I want to stay."

"Are you crazy? What nonsense is this, all of a sudden? This is no place for humans, especially for you. Who do you think you are? If you stay, they'll throw you in Hell immediately."

"Brrrr. . . . Let's go . . . let's go," Mredah burst out, suddenly in a great hurry.

And so they left. The return journey was smooth, swift and easy. His face glowing with satisfaction, Bhima strode along, bearing the winged goblet of the Tirta Amrta, while Twalen and Mredah kept up a steady stream of chatter. Their words flew about in all directions, as if each were talking to himself about this and that, about all that had transpired both in Hell and in Heaven. Bhima maintained his usual silence. Finally they reached the familiar landscape of the Pandawa kingdom, and as they made their entry into the palace, a magnificent celebration began.

During the festivities, King Pandu and Dewi Madri received the water of eternal life. After only a few sips, the royal couple rose with the greatest agility and grace. No one could utter a word. The entire royal family was too moved to speak. Only Twalen and Mredah had not lost their tongues.

"Only a few sips! Who's going to drink the rest?" Mredah asked his father.

"Be quiet, I say!" Twalen scolded. Then he added, as if to himself, "Where *are* they going to store it? Who's going to drink what's left?"

Pandu and Madri were now ready to leave for Heaven. They had undergone so many experiences that now, in their purified condition, they could see the truth about life in a way they had never anticipated. In their last minutes together, they shared their newly discovered insights with Kunti, their sons and the clowns.

"Life is a timeless treasure," they said softly and tenderly. "There is no beginning and no end to it. Harmony is the result of a day embracing three things: work and learning and recreation. Dreams are very important, too. You must cherish them."

Unlike ordinary departures, those final moments of the family's reunion were filled with peace and joy. When Pandu and Madri disappeared in the direction of Heaven, Twalen and Mredah did not realize it. They could not take their eyes off the goblet of holy water, and their thoughts were buried in some secret dream of immortality. As they stared at the water, they marveled at its purity; it was so clear they could see every vein in the gold at the bottom of the goblet. Staring thus—immersing themselves, as it were, in the miraculous water—they became hypnotized. Then, overwhelmed by their powers of imagination, they watched the liquid's surface widen until they thought they had entered a land made of gold, a land they immediately recognized as Heaven itself. Gold spread out in all directions, glittering more brightly than the sun itself. In their hypnotic dream state, they gazed silently.

They saw that Pandu and Madri had already reached Heaven and were now resting among the elect of the southern regions. The South was the dwelling place of all those who had always been devoted to the gods, those who had faithfully placed offerings on the shrines and been generous with priests.

While Twalen's attention was still drawn to those regions, Mredah's eyes drifted off toward the western part of Heaven.

"The West seems to be empty," he thought.

Little Mredah was right, because the West was the least inhabited part of Heaven. Here were the souls of those who had always been honest with others as well as with themselves. Among the few elect, there were the souls of men who had spent their free time observing the colors and movements of nature and had then represented their impressions through the medium of painting for the visual pleasure of the gods. Accompanying them were masters of stone and wood carving who had devoted all their leisure hours to decorating palaces and temples. Here also dwelt the souls of those wise men, gifted in the art of listening and remembering, who had transcribed the holy scriptures and had recounted innumerable instructive legends about animals and men. And next to them resided the musicians and poets who had filled the world with melodious sounds dedicated to the gods.

At this point, little Mredah, who was about to say something, was stopped by Twalen, who held his finger to his mouth as a gesture of silence.

"Listen . . . ," said Twalen, "listen. . . ."

A beautiful melody, coming from the northern region of Heaven, filled their ears. It enveloped them with such power that they both closed their eyes in order to concentrate and not miss even a single word.

A king and a queen
Who meditate
Will find the wisdom to protect
The people of their realm.

A king and a queen
Who love each other
And never feel old
Will find the strength
To foster love
Among the people of their realm.

A king and a queen
Who sacrifice to all the gods
Will find the power to save
The people of their realm.

To Heaven they will go,
This king and queen.

190

As the melody faded into the distance, King Pandu and Dewi Madri had already reached the East.

Twalen and Mredah had always been told that the East of Heaven was an extraordinary place, crowded with the souls of those who had always been satisfied with whatever they had, be it small or great. But all the clowns could see were the souls of those who had regularly practiced fasting, meditation and yoga.

Suddenly, something truly unusual happened: Sanghyang Acintya, the god of all gods, the ultimate force embracing all forces, appeared. Slim and graceful, tall and agile, he looked like a dancer suspended motionless in midair. He glowed, shimmering in the glory of his halo. The East was none other than his own abode.

"The god Acintya . . . ," the clowns whispered, and they bowed with the utmost reverence.

The god welcomed Pandu and Madri with a gesture that was like a long wave of warm water flowing over cold skin. He invited them to sit down and make themselves at home. So they did.

Then, to their great surprise, Twalen and Mredah noticed that the goblet of the Tirta Amrta, the water of immortality, was set between King Pandu and Dewi Madri in Heaven. Father and son stared at the goblet, and then they opened their eyes—only to discover that they had never left the palace at all. They were still in the throne room. Everyone else had left. They shook their heads. Their eyes opened even wider. In utter amazement they realized that what had so captured their imagination was nothing more than a brass bowl filled with ordinary drinking water.

❖

NOTES

1 The best source of information regarding the caste system of Bali is Hildred and Clifford Geertz, *Kinship in Bali*, University of Chicago Press, Chicago and London, 1975.

2 Ibid.

3 The Balinese language replaces the Sanskrit "v" sound with "w": Kauravas, for example, the Balinese spell Korawas; Svarga is Swarga; Siva is Siwa; Pandava is Pandawa, and so on.

4 C. P. Roy, *The Mahabharata*, vol. 12, Oriental Publishing Co., Calcutta, 1928, p. 292.

5 Clifford Geertz, *Negara*, Princeton University Press, Princeton, N.J., 1980, pp. 87–88.

6 Roy, op. cit., pp. 281–284.

7 *Ni Djah Tantri* is the Javano-Balinese version of the Indian *Pancatantra*, the source for the tales of *One Thousand and One Nights*. The legend goes that a king demands a fresh virgin every night to satisfy his appetite till a particularly gifted girl, in this case Tantri (Scheherazade), succeeds in so captivating the king with her unfinished tales that he lives on night after night waiting in vain for an end. At last the king realizes she has become indispensable to him, and he makes her his wife. Kertha Gosa's bottom row of panels, beginning from the eastern side, depicts five such tales.

8 The *Adiparwa* stories are an offshoot of the first book of the *Mahabharata*. Among other things, they narrate myths of creation. At Kertha Gosa, they inspire the story of Garuda, the sacred bird of Vishnu, his birth and legendary theft of the water of immortality from the gods.

9 This calendar appears to have been added after the earthquake that shook Klungkung in 1917. This is likely because it gives particular emphasis to the significance of earthquakes in relation to each month of the year. Twelve gods appear on the calendar, each protecting his own month and warning the inhabitants of earth of coming events. This is to remind mankind that nature has its cosmic balance and will forever strive to maintain it. Each god is, in effect, a spokesman on behalf of nature.

10 Much leeway should be given to dates. The Balinese, in general, are not in the habit of keeping precise dates; and in any case, their calendar system differs from that of the West. As sources for dates I have used Dr. Willard A. Hanna's *Bali Profile: People, Events, Circumstances (1001–1976)*, and *Sejarah Bali* by Nyoka, the standard history handbook distributed for primary and secondary school reading in Bali. Although its dates might not be entirely accurate, I have chosen the latter simply because it is what the young people of Bali are being taught to believe.

11 The best source of information on Klungkung and the history of its palace is *Negara* by Clifford Geertz, op. cit.

12 Anak Agung Gdé Pameregan, *Gaguritan Padem Warak*, Bali, 1842.

13 The Pura Dalem ("temple of the dead") Paminggékan of Bangli; the Pura Dalem of Gianyar; and the Pura Dalem Bale Agung of Tabanan.

14 The reproductions in this book show the ceiling before the replacement of these eight panels.

15 The tooth-filing ceremony, an important rite of passage in Bali, takes place in late adolescence or at marriage. Its purpose is to diminish the six most important human passions—lust, anger, jealousy, greed, intoxication, confusion—by filing down the six upper canine teeth and incisors to a uniform line. Unfiled teeth are symbolic of aggression, and tradition says that a person should not enter Swarga looking like a demon.

16 In Bali this black-and-white material has sacred connotations, for it is believed to carry protective powers. One can see it very often as part of the normal "landscape" in a variety of contexts: around the *gamelan* instruments when not in use; around the stone guardian figures at the entrance of temples; around the bodies of the Balinese themselves during festivities, etc. White represents powers that favor man's spiritual development, while black signifies the powers that retard or oppose this development. (Sometimes, as in the clown Mredah's case, red replaces black.)

BIBLIOGRAPHY

Artaud, Antonin. *The Theater and Its Double*, New York, 1958.

Bateson, G., and Margaret Mead. *Balinese Character: A Photographic Analysis*, New York, 1942.

Baum, Vicki. *A Tale from Bali*, London, 1937.

Belo, Jane. *Trance in Bali*, New York, 1960.

——. *Traditional Balinese Culture*, New York, London, 1970.

Black, Star, and Willard A. Hanna. *Bali*, Singapore, 1983.

Bodrogi, T. *L'Art de l'Indonésie*, Budapest, Paris, 1972.

Boon, James. *The Anthropological Romance of Bali*, Cambridge, London, New York, Melbourne, 1977.

Brandon, J. R. *On Thrones of Gold: Three Javanese Shadow Plays*, Cambridge, Mass., 1970.

Buitenen, J.A.B. van. *The Mahabharata*, Chicago, London, 1973.

Chandra, M. *New Documents of Jaina Painting*, Bombay, 1975.

Coomaraswamy, A. K. *History of Indian and Indonesian Art*, New York, 1965.

Covarrubias, Miguel. *Island of Bali*, New York, 1936.

Crawford, John. "On the Existence of the Hindu Religion in the Island of Bali," *Asiatick Researches*, 13 (1820): 128–170.

Daniel, Ana. *Bali: Behind the Mask*, New York, 1981.

Das Gupta, R. P. *Crime and Punishment in Ancient India*, Sonarpur Varanasi, 1973.

de Bary, W. T. *Sources of Indian Tradition*, New York, 1958.

Dehejia, V. *Living and Dying*, New Delhi, 1979.

de Kleen, Tyra. *Mudras: The Ritual Hand Poses of the Buddha Priests and the Shiva Priests of Bali*, London, 1924.

de Zoete, B., and Walter Spies, *Dance and Drama in Bali*, London, 1938.

Forge, Anthony. *Balinese Traditional Painting*, Sydney, 1978.

Friedrich, R. *The Civilization and Culture of Bali*, Calcutta, 1959.

Friend, Donald. *The Cosmic Turtle*, Bali, 1978.

Geertz, Clifford. *Negara*, Princeton, N.J., 1980.

——. *The Interpretation of Cultures*, New York, 1973.

Geertz, H., and Clifford Geertz. *Kinship in Bali*, Chicago, London, 1975.

Ginarsa, K. *Gambar Lambang* [Pictorial Symbols], Bali, 1971.

Gorer, G. *Bali and Angkor, or Looking at Life and Death*, Boston, 1936.

Gralapp, L. W. *Balinese Painting*, Colorado Springs, 1961.

——. *Balinese Painting and the Wayang Tradition*, Artibus Asiae, vol. 29, Ascona, 1967.

Grof, S., and Christina Grof. *Beyond Death*, London, 1980.

Hanna, Willard A. *Bali Profile: People, Events, Circumstances (1001–1976)*, Hanover, N.H., 1976.

Herman, A. L. *The Problem of Evil in Indian Thought*, New Delhi, 1976.

Holt, C. *Art in Indonesia: Continuities and Change*, Ithaca, N.Y., 1967.

Hughes, Robert. *Heaven and Hell in Western Art*, New York, 1968.

Kane, P. V. *History of Dharmasastra*, vol. 4, Poona, 1973.

K'tut, Tantri. *Revolt in Paradise*, New York, 1960.

Larivière, R. W. *The Divyatattva of Raghunandana Bhattacarya: Ordeals in Classical Hindu Law*, New Delhi, 1981.

Law, B. C. *The Buddhist Conception of Spirits*, Sonarpur Varanasi, 1974.

McPhee, Colin. *Music in Bali: A Study in Form and Instrumental Organization in Balinese Orchestral Music*, New Haven, London, 1966.

Mason, Victor. *The Haughty Toad and Other Balinese Stories*, Sydney, 1976.

Nyoka, *Sejarah Bali* [History of Bali], Bali, 1975.

Ramseyer, U. *The Art and Culture of Bali*, Oxford, 1977.

Rhodius, H., and John Darling. *Walter Spies and Balinese Art*, Amsterdam, 1980.

Rigmodis Hinzler, H. I. *Bhima Swarga in Balinese Wayang*, Verhandenlingen, vol. 90, Leiden, 1979.

Roy, C. P. *The Mahabharata*, vol. 12, Calcutta, 1928.

Sivananda, Sri S. *What Becomes of the Soul after Death*, The Divine Life Society, India, 1972.

Stuart-Fox, D. *The Art of Balinese Offering*, Jogjakarta, 1974.

——. *Once a Century: Pura Besakih and the Eka Dasa Rudra Festival*, Jakarta, 1982.

Stutterheim, Willem F. *Indian Influences in Old Balinese Art*, London, 1935.

Sweeney, A. *Malay Shadow Puppets*, London, 1972.

Swellengrebel, J. L. *Bali: Studies in Life, Thought and Ritual*, The Hague, 1960.

Ulbricht, U. *Wayang Purwa: Shadows of the Past*, Oxford, Kuala Lumpur, 1972.

Vansina, Jan. *Oral Tradition: A Study in Historical Methodology*, Chicago, 1961.

Vitsaxis, V. *Plato and the Upanishads*, New Delhi, 1977.

GLOSSARY

agung great, big.

Airlangga eleventh-century Javanese king.

alus refined in terms of behavior, craftmanship, and/or performance; opposite of *kasar*.

ancur fish-derived gelatin glue used in preparation of cloth and colors in traditional *wayang*-style painting.

Arjuna one of the five Pandawa brothers (the third in line) of the *Mahabharata* epic; a model of physical beauty, self-mastery and dedication.

Aswins twin gods and heavenly fathers of Nakula and Sahadewa, the Pandawa twins born of Madri, second wife of King Pandu.

atal Balinese type of clay.

bale raised platform building covered with a roof, constructed partly of masonry and partly of wood.

bale Kambang floating pavilion.

banci literally, "hermaphrodite"; colloquial for homosexual or transvestite.

banjar social and political village council.

banyan; waringin the huge Indian fig tree, *Ficus bengalensis*.

baris warrior dance, highly stylized and performed only by men.

Batavia former name for Indonesian city of Jakarta.

Bayu Bhima's heavenly father, the god of wind and air.

Bharata ethnic name of North Indian people in the *Mahabharata*.

bhatara title given to a god.

Bhima one of the five Pandawa brothers (the second in line) of the *Mahabharata* epic; a model of prodigious strength and courage; jovial when in a good mood but abusive when his passion is aroused; a superman of action, not of words.

bhuta demon, obnoxious spirit.

Brahma the "creator," one of the gods of the Hindu trinity.

brahmana highest, priestly class of the *triwangsa*, the Hindu caste system of Bali *(brahmana, satria* and *wesia)*; a *brahman* is a member of this caste.

Buginese ethnic group of South Sulawesi.

cokorda male title among the *satria* caste of Bali.

dalang the puppet player of the shadow theater, regarded as a priest with exorcist powers.

Delem retainer-clown of Swarga, and older brother of Sangut; an incurable optimist and braggart.

dewa divinity, god; also male title among the *satria* caste of Bali.

Dewa Agung title of the ruler of Gelgel and later Klungkung (literally, "the highest god").

dewi divinity, goddess.

Dewi Sri goddess of rice and fertility.

Dharma god of virtue; also *dharma*, an individual's duty fulfilled by observance of custom and law.

Dharmawangsa Balinese alternative name of Yudhisthira, the eldest Pandawa brother.

dukun; balian folk healer; both herbal doctor and practitioner of magic.

Durga goddess of death and destruction; consort of Siwa.

gamelan generic term in Bali and Java for orchestras composed of and music played with percussion instruments such as gongs, drums, metallophones, etc.

Gana elephant-headed son of Siwa.

Gedong Kirtya library of palm-leaf *(lontar)* manuscripts in Singaraja, Bali.

gecko lizard that hides in Balinese houses; its presence is revealed by intermittent, hiccuplike sounds varying in number, to which the Balinese superstitiously attach special meaning.

Gelgel Balinese kingdom of the fifteenth to seventeenth century.

gender-wayang musical ensemble of the shadow theater, comprising four musicians, each playing a ten-key metallophone with bamboo resonators.

gusti male title among the *wesia* caste of Bali.

Hanuman white monkey of the *Ramayana* epic.

ida bagus male title among the *brahmana* caste of Bali.

ider-ider long, narrow *wayang*-style paintings hung around the eaves of temple shrines.

Indra	god of thunder and rain.
istri	wife.
Istri Lui	honorific for the "best wife."
Jogormanik	the minister-judge of Hell, one of the most popular characters in Balinese folklore.
kain	Balinese cloth worn by men and women, wrapped around the body much like a *sarong*.
kain poleng	black-and-white checked cloth worn by Bhima, Twalen and Hanuman; its pattern conveys magic power. Nowadays, it is used by the Balinese as protective garb against evil influences.
kaiu curiga	dagger *(kris)* tree in Hell.
kakayonan	the cosmic tree, figure of the *wayang* puppet theater.
Kamasan	local center for painters in the traditional *wayang* style, near the town of Klungkung.
Kanda Empat	four older "brothers" or "sisters," spiritual companions of a man or woman from conception until death.
karma	the spiritual force generated by a person's actions, believed in Hinduism and Buddhism to perpetuate transmigration and in its ethical consequence to determine one's destiny in a subsequent existence.
kasar	crude, unrefined, ungracious, coarse, impolite; anything badly made or performed; opposite of *alus*.
Kauravas	cousins and bitter enemies of the Pandawas in the *Mahabharata* epic.
Kawah Blegede	the silent crater of Hell, a vast lake of lava.
Kawi	ancient Javanese language containing Sanskrit derivations; literally, "to speak in comparison." This is the mode in which poetry is created, comparisons being the ornaments of poetry.
kencu	imported Chinese vermilion used as base for the red color of *wayang* paintings.
kerthas	Balinese priests acting as judges.
ketu	form of headdress used by the Pandawa queen Kunti and by priests in *wayang* paintings.
Klungkung	former royal capital of Bali and seat of the Dewa Agung, the highest Balinese royal title.
kris	Malay and Indonesian double-edged dagger, symbol of masculine strength; usually a serpentine blade believed to be endowed with magical power.
kulit	buffalo hide.
kulkul	wooden signal drum.
Kunti	first wife of King Pandu and mother of the three older Pandawa brothers (Yudhisthira, Bhima and Arjuna).
legong	highly stylized dance performed by prepubescent girls.
lontar	the palmirah palm, whose leaves are used for making mats, baskets and paper; also a term referring to sacred books made from these leaves, dried and etched with a sharp point and then bound together.
Madri	second wife of King Pandu and mother of the two youngest Pandawa brothers (Nakula and Sahadewa).
Mahabharata	Indian epic narrating the battle between the Pandawa and the Kaurava brothers.
Majapahit	great Javanese kingdom of the thirteenth to fifteenth century.
malpal	position in *baris* dance and in *topeng:* turned-out thigh with knee and foot raised and bent.
mata kranjang	"basket eyes"; term used for a person of erratic, unfocused behavior.
medang	substance found in the trunk of bamboo trees.
meru	multiroofed pagoda or shrine.
Mredah	retainer-clown of the Pandawas; in the south of Bali, believed to be Twalen's son, while in the north regarded as his younger brother.
mudra	sacred ritual gesture.
Nakula	one of the five Pandawa brothers. With his brother Sahadewa, known for his ability to solve problems and carry out plans, for his wisdom paired with transcendental knowledge, clairvoyance and magic power.
padanda	*brahmana* high priest (plural, *pedanda*).
Pandawas	collective name for the sons of Pandu, the five heroes of the *Mahabharata:* Yudhisthira, Bhima, Arjuna, Nakula and Sahadewa, brothers of semidivine origin.

Pandu	reputed father of the five Pandawa brothers.
parwa	section of the *Mahabharata* epic.
prada	gold leaf applied to *wayang* paintings.
prasasti	sacred *lontar* containing the ancient history of a particular village or family.
puputan	ceremonial death of a warrior-king; literally, "a fight to the end."
puri	palace of a nobleman.
Puri Semara Pura	the palace of Klungkung; literally, "place of love, peace and tranquillity."
raja	a Hindu prince or local potentate (Sanskrit, "king").
Ramayana	Indian epic of Rama and Sita.
Sahadewa	one of the five Pandawa brothers, twin brother of Nakula.
sakti	magical and mystical power of a human, animal or object.
Sanghyang Acintya	deity symbolizing extreme unity. Acintya has no shrines or observances but is central to the Balinese pantheon.
Sangut	retainer-clown of Swarga, and Delem's brother; a pessimist and pacifist at heart.
Sarayu	mythical river.
sarong	garment worn on lower half of the body.
sate	local dish consisting of chunks of meat or special meat paste on a skewer, grilled over an open flame.
satria	second highest Hindu caste, comprising warriors and nobles.
Siwa	the great Hindu god, the supreme god of the Balinese pantheon.
Somba Wesi	the Iron Gate, a torture mechanism in Hell; literally, the "flexible iron."
sudra	anyone in Bali who is not a member of the *triwangsa* caste system of the three high castes; generally comprising farmers and other manual laborers.
Suratma	the record-keeper of Hell.
Surya	sun-god.
Swarga	abode of the gods; general term for the afterlife and world of the dead.
Tambra Goh Muka	enormous cauldron with cowhead handles in Hell.
Tirta Amrta	water of immortality (tirta, "water"; amrta, "freedom from death").
Togtogsil	monstrous one-eyed demon of Hell.
topeng	mask; masked dance drama.
"Tri kaya pari suddha"	Balinese proverb: "Think, speak, and do."
triwangsa	collective name for the three high Hindu castes of Bali *(brahmana, satria* and *wesia).*
tuak	palm wine.
Twalen	retainer-clown of the Pandawas, father (or older brother) of Mredah. He is often thought of as controlling the outcome of actions of his nominal superiors, ensuring that good triumphs. He is the ideal of *sudra* (layman's) inspiration, for he manages to control events without seeking the pinnacles of refined behavior and ostentatious power that belong by birth only to members of the *triwangsa*. Regarded as the progenitor of the common people, he is their voice, their apologist, their champion.
ushada	Balinese *lontar* of medical lore.
Vishnu	the "preserver," one of the gods of the Hindu trinity.
Vyasa	compiler of the epic *Mahabharata*.
wayang	puppet figure (literally, "shadow").
wayang kulit	shadow-puppet theater of Java and Bali.
wesia	third highest Hindu caste, comprising merchants and businessmen.
Yama	god of departed souls and supreme master of Hell.
Yamaloka	Yama's dwelling; Hell (loka, "place").
Yudhisthira	one of the five Pandawa brothers (the eldest) of the *Mahabharata*, a model of dispassionate judgment and unswerving rectitude; in Bali, also known as Dharmawangsa.

❖

Designed by Martine Bruel

Set in Clearface Regular, Bold and Heavy (ITC) by
Hamilton Phototype

Separations, printing and binding by Tien Wah Press, Ltd.